Vanguard of a New World

Sudbury Valley School's Staff at the Half-Century Mark

Interviews by Hanna Greenberg
and Mimsy Sadofsky

*"It was creating a new world, and we were
strangers in the world that we were creating."*

Sudbury Valley School Press®

This book is dedicated
to the members of the
Sudbury Valley School community
1968–2018

Vanguard of a New World

Sudbury Valley School's Staff at the Half Century Mark

Interviews by Hanna Greenberg and Mimsy Sadofsky

Prefatory Note

Fifty years have passed since Sudbury Valley School was established. Thousands of students have come and gone, but throughout those years, the school has been served by a staff that has worked to maintain the integrity of its ideals and practices.

I thought it would be interesting and illuminating to hear the personal stories of the current staff about their experiences. So I interviewed them, and recorded their answers—except for myself and Danny, who were interviewed by Mimsy.

Hanna Greenberg

June 5, 2018

Scott Gray

"If you want a person to really be able to take what life brings them, you've got to make sure that they feel power over their own lives, control over their own lives from day one."

Hanna: Scott, you came to the school when you were ten years old. Why did you come here?

Scott: Like so many people, I came here because I had trouble, because I could not stand school, and they could not stand me. So I think it was to everyone's benefit for me to come here.

Hanna: Was it difficult for your parents, philosophically?

Scott: I think so. I think it was very difficult. Part of it is that the school philosophically is deeper and harder to understand than it can appear. I think my father thought he knew what the school was about, and he didn't really. And it took him some time to be comfortable with my being here. My mother had the sort of wisdom to say that she didn't need to know what it was about if her little boy was happy.

Hanna: I know this will embarrass you, but you were obviously very intelligent and quite precocious in understanding the world around you. And especially sensitive to other people's coercion or trying to get at your life. You're pretty confident about your own self. That's probably the way you were raised: you didn't lose your belief that you can be the master of your life within your family. But it's interesting to me that other parents, who have a kid who is not so successful academically, worry because they think the way to success is to succeed in school. With you we have parents who worry about their successful kid. So you were so unhappy they just let you come here.

Scott: Well, partly because it was in the early '80s, and partly because of who they were individually, I don't think that it was as hard for them to accept that this would be okay. My father was, without question, an academic superstar but most of his life he was in humble surroundings in small towns—in Minnesota, and in Vermont—working-class areas, and he never had any discomfort about that. I think that to the extent he cared about academia, he had no concerns about learning academics according to one's own likes on one's own. Because that's what he did, his interests drew him when they drew him.

Hanna: So, you came here, and you think you understood the school as a ten year old?

Scott: Well, certainly not. I understood what it wasn't. And that was enough. It was not a place where I was going to be made not only to do what others were telling me but made to thank them for it.

Hanna: What did you do all day when you were ten?

Scott: When I first came to school, in 1980, I remember very vividly that this school made one big mistake back in those days, which we have since corrected—we corrected, actually, the first year I came to work as a staff member; but I remember very vividly that when I came and for years after that, the staff at the start of the year would post signs and sign-up sheets that said: here's the class I'm able to teach if people want it.

Most staff had something like that on the bulletin board. And I remember I was here in the school that all I knew for sure is that this was better than the place that I left, and I had to hang onto it. I had to find a way to fit it and make my way here. And when you see a big list from the adults and leaders in the community that you're joining, you say: well, that's how you do it. And I signed up right away for four classes, including Hanna Greenberg's chemistry class. I'll take this opportunity to say thank goodness we got rid of that, because it was misleading, it was frightening, it was not what the school was about. It was the wrong introduction to the school to walk in and see those signs on that board.

Hanna: Why do you think we did it?

Scott: I think you did it for a lot of reasons. For one, the school was young, and it had not quite shaken out in the culture that everyone really, really, really does get to know each other and know what they are capable of and do. For another, I think that it was done because it came from the idea of sort of the open community in which academia could be pursued as an aside. In a town of 30,000, someone would have to post it somewhere who's able to be a tutor in this or that or the other thing.

Hanna: So you are ten years and you signed up, how long did you survive classes?

Scott: Well, I'll tell you what happened. I was I think two or three weeks on, I was doing all my homework and studiously taking my notes and devoting an hour each day to sitting with those notes, seeing them as the price to be here. And one day, I've got all my papers laid out, and a staff member, Joan Rubin, came up to me and posed a simple question. I wish I could match her tone because this question was not just the word, it was the tone. She just looked and said: "Why?" There was a presumption in her tone that said: There's nothing wrong with it, but presumably you have a reason, you wouldn't do it without a reason—that told me that external reasons, this idea that I'm going to fit into this society, that this is how you get along here, was not true. And that it was okay to just drop it. I never went back to any of those classes. That was the end.

Hanna: So, what did you do? Did you play outside?

Scott: Yes. Also the first year I spent a lot of time sitting in every corner of the school, trying to understand what the different groups of kids were doing I formed friendships but I liked to know what other groups of people were doing. So, when I wasn't playing with the guys that I sort of saw as my buddies, I would go somewhere else and be on the fringes of the conversation and sometimes join it to a greater or lesser extent.

Hanna: Did you enjoy the age-mixing here?

Scott: Oh absolutely. One of the most important realizations for me came from your son, Michael, who was probably seventeen. I asked for his help to certify me for the darkroom and to show me how to use it. Over the course of working with him, he showed such genuine interest in me and my opinions and my thoughts, while sharing his opinions and thoughts, in a way that can be described by no other word than friendship. The reality that my age had nothing to do with our conversations, had nothing to do with his attitude towards me, had a huge impact on me: to realize that he was ready to take anyone seriously, including this new kid who was just over half his age, and treat them as human. That was really an education in this school.

It was not necessarily that I did not like adults, it was that I assumed that adults always had an agenda; no matter how hard they tried to bury it, they had it somewhere.

Hanna: But that did not extend to the teenagers.

Scott: No. I never felt that was an issue.

Hanna: When you left you were ready to go. Were you then thinking of maybe one day coming to be staff?

Scott: I was. I wrote about it in my thesis (when we had theses). It was mentioned as an aside. I wrote at length that I did not know what to expect in my life, that I understood that life unfolds in so many ways, and there's so much to discover about yourself and the world, and so much change that happens, that there was no reasonable way for me to say what job I might get. But that among the jobs I listed, I said I could picture myself coming back here.

Hanna: That's very interesting. I was thinking that you wanted to study neuroscience or some kind of psychology based on biology.

Scott: I actually attended college for political science with an interest in the historical angle, but Boston College was the wrong place to choose for the historical angle. Boston College prepares people for pre-law and local politics. But by dabbling in the theology department and the history department I worked it out.

I learned an awful lot about Jesuits. One of my best friends is a professor and was a middle-aged priest named Father Madigan who I felt very close to. I still remember one semester he complained to me: "I don't know why no one does the reading."

Hanna: So between the age of ten and eighteen you didn't do any academics—not at home or here—at least no taking of tests, preparing for tests, no writing unless you wanted to do it on your own, no having somebody critique your writing and probably not doing algebra, etc. Did you take SATs?

Scott: I did.

Hanna: Did you do well?

Scott: Well, I did not aim to do better than the university I was applying to. I admit I had a very direct aim. I took the sample SAT books, gave myself a sample test, and said okay how do I compare to the high end of the range for acceptance to the university I want to attend. I discovered my verbal was great, I don't need to worry about that. My math, I could see exactly what kinds of questions that were really foreign to me, so I saw what to do. I circled the questions I had problems with, I talked to David Gould.

He was a staff member here, and I said, "I've got a couple weeks till my test and I'd like to learn this. I've taken the sample test and I've got some questions. How is one expected to calculate this, or what is that asking?" He kind of went through it with me. Between his advice and a math book, I was able to look everything up with direction about what I was looking for, really mostly trigonometry. And then I took another sample test, it looked fine and I went back to David and said: what can I spruce up here?

Hanna: Do you remember Peter Shirley? Peter Shirley told me I want to take the SATs, and I said "Peter, you have to really study for a few months." He said, "I don't." I said, "How come?" He said, "The answer is in the question." I said, "That's usually not the question they ask you." A few months later he took the SATs. He called me on a Saturday night. I said, "Peter, what happened?" He said, "I think you'll be very happy to hear that I got a very high score on my math." So, what is it about you kids who go to Sudbury Valley? Is it confidence, is it arrogance, what is it? What is it? You never do any math, and you think in two weeks you can just learn what you need?

Scott: Other alumni and I have had this conversation a lot. I'm pretty convinced there's a few things at work. The first is they don't take it too seriously. If you go in to any test thinking it's the end of the world, you're never going to be able to pass it. You're going to be shitting bricks, you're going to be so full of anxiety that you're not going to be able to do it. You've got to be able to face it with a degree of seriousness but with a degree of humor. Just understand that it is what it is, and it's nothing more than that.

Hanna: And at the age of seventeen, kids have that wisdom?

Scott: People develop that wisdom naturally any place they're not treated like animals in a cage. When you spend your whole day without any time that's your own, without any power over yourself, it's hard to take anything as a joke. If you want a person to really be able to take what life brings them, you've got to make sure that they feel power over their own lives, control over their own lives from day one.

Hanna: That's what the little kids feel.

Scott: Absolutely.

Hanna: But you came when you were ten. How long did it take you to get there?

Scott: I was helped a little bit by the fact that, as my friend Hanna Greenberg likes to say, this is a relatively easy school for rebels because they've managed to maintain their person over incredible odds.

So, I came having protected myself. But what really did take me time was to trust the adults. I remember very vividly that my first year in this school, I wasted so much time attending School Meetings that I had zero interest in because I was watching for when the staff pulled the strings. I was sure that was going on there. Really it took over a year before I said okay, I guess that this is for real, that this is an actual debate—no one's pulling punches, no one's hiding their opinions. The staff certainly have opinions on things and share them but they're not overbearing. And that was very significant.

Hanna: Scott, did you read any of our literature, or when you came to the enrollment interview, did you listen to the answers? How does a kid come here and figure out the philosophy?

Scott: Every kid is different, obviously, but I think for most kids it's hard to walk into this place and not feel a calling—and also for most adults who have not already killed whatever remains in them of their infancy, I think it's hard to come here as a young person and not feel something tugging at you that you've missed, and you haven't had for a long time.

Hanna: Did it help you that the staff were on a first name basis? Was that significant to you?

Scott: What was significant is not that they were first names, but that we were all on an equal footing. If I had been Mr. Gray and you had been Ms. Greenberg, it would have been equal. It's not the fact that it was casual: that it was the same standard either way is what made it good.

Hanna: Did you feel respected?

Scott: No question. That was vitally important. I'm not alone in that. This is what any kid I've ever met hungers for in this society.

Hanna: How do you define respect?

Scott: Respect is faith that the person can handle their own affairs.

Hanna: How long do you think it takes a kid, just from observation? A year?

Scott: I think a year's about how long it takes, but I've been here now for 38 years, and I still learn more about this school and what it is to be here.

Hanna: You were a young man of eighteen. Your father is a professor, your mother is extremely well-educated and intellectual and a poet, I believe. And she had a great influence on you. You were very close. All I had to do is meet your mother, Anita, to know that she was a power intellectually, right? You began going to college; did you enjoy it?

Scott: Well, no. I was in a funny kind of position. I sort of knew I wouldn't enjoy it. My terms for going to college were: I was not going to pay for the privilege of going to college. And I was not going to ask my parents for money. I was going to get a full scholarship.

Hanna: But you didn't have to because your father was a professor in the college that you went to.

Scott: That's right. So I was not going to look at any other school than the school that I could go to without paying. They certainly offered to pay. But I wanted to be in control of my own life to the extent that I could. And if I went to college, this transformative moment in so many people's lives, on my parents' dime, at the point in my life that I'm claiming I can take care of myself from here on, it just would not have felt right to me.

That's a peculiarity in me. I worry about being indebted to people a lot. I don't think there's anything wrong with it, I just couldn't picture myself putting my parents in debt for something that was supposedly for my future.

Hanna: But they probably had a college fund from the day you were born.

Scott: Well, if they did, then they should have saved it for something more useful.

I went to college believing that I could, with the expense of the room and board and everything else that it takes to go to college, have educated myself better in four years on my own. Let me put it this way: I was not going to ask my parents to pay for something that I didn't believe in, that was the problem. I went to college saying to myself—I guess it was out of pride—that I always want to be clear of this style of education, but I don't want, as I go through life, to have people say: oh, sour grapes, you didn't go, you couldn't understand. So I went.

Hanna: Was it all the school's influence, or you had your own perception?

Scott: The school certainly strengthened and gave me more practical arguments in terms of what I saw in my day-to-day life for what my gut said when I was a kid.

Hanna: At that age, what did you want to do when you grew up?

Scott: There were endless possibilities, but I thought that the likely idea was to be a professor of political history. In particular, I was very interested in the politics of the ancient world, of the Bronze Age, of the actual political dynamic in the Mesopotamia Valley in between them and the kingdom of Egypt.

Hanna: So you might have gone to college because that was a secure idea. Did you make friends in college?

Scott: Yes.

Hanna: Was that an important part for you?

Scott: Probably not that important for me, actually. Which is one reason that college wasn't that important for me. For a lot of people, going to college is very important because they want to be close friends with a lot of people going through the same things they are. For me, I felt I had a lot of friends in college but some of my closest were not people at all like me. They were professors.

Hanna: You were born a good writer. Did you improve your writing in college?

Scott: My writing has certainly improved over the years, but I think the four years I was in college it basically stayed at a standstill.

Hanna: Did you feel like you were wasting your time?

Scott: I did, but I feel like I signed up to waste my time.

Hanna: What did you do after you graduated?

Scott: I went on to a lot of things. I started a couple different small businesses. In sequence. I think it was at the same time, actually, when I was doing computer consulting for a lot of people, and I also started a retail store—a game store.

Hanna: Aren't you one of the kids who introduced the computer to the school?

Scott: A number of kids in the school had some access to computers here and at home—or in my case at Boston College where my father worked. I worked with the big machine there. And with the personal computer kind of exploding on the scene, it was something that a lot of the kids were very interested in. We did a lot of fundraising and we bought an Apple II.

Hanna: So by the time you're eighteen you're pretty advanced.

Scott: I was reasonably good at what I was doing with it, yes.

Hanna: Was it all self-taught?

Scott: At the time there were not a whole lot of other options.

Hanna: So you did some consulting. How did people come to you? How did you get clients?

Scott: Word-of-mouth was helpful. After getting a couple jobs, suddenly everyone who I worked for, who I did a good job for, had a friend who also needed help. And sometimes it was personal, getting people's own computers set up and so forth. But more often it was industrial, getting a business set up that wanted help, initial computer networking, getting cash registers logging in to a local server in some way or another, that kind of thing.

Hanna: But you weren't thinking of Sudbury Valley at the time.

Scott: Well, I couldn't stop thinking about Sudbury Valley. I maintained my relationship with the school by joining the Board of Trustees as soon as I left the school. So it gave me an excuse to come on campus when I wanted, and I made use of it. I cared about the school.

Hanna: Did you have a car?

Scott: I did, yes. Working as I was, consulting for a lot of different people, I needed a car. I needed to be able to go to New Hampshire, I needed to go to the western part of the State.

Hanna: You made a lot of money doing your consulting?

Scott: I don't think I made that much money.

Hanna: Didn't you make more money than we did here at the school as staff?

Scott: At that time, yes—no question.

Hanna: On one hand you want to be independent of your parents and you also like to buy books and maybe computers, so money was important.

Scott: Money is always important.

Hanna: When did it come to your head that it might be worthwhile to work here, aside from the fact that our salaries were not fantastic?

Scott: Well, recompense comes in all kinds of forms. There were a few factors. It was a concert of things, one of which is that this school and what this school is about has always been not just useful for me, but deeply intellectually interesting for me. It wasn't just that I was a beneficiary of the way that the school operated, but that I was actually deeply interested in questions of how to let people be independent and how to help people keep their independence in life.

Hanna: Did you like children?

Scott: Yes, absolutely.

Hanna: So you wanted to do it for children?

Scott: Well, I think that I wanted to do it for anyone, which was one reason I also worked at the VA Hospital; I worked part-time with a professor who was working at Harvard in theory of mind studies at that hospital.

Hanna: Injured people or PTSD?

Scott: We studied people who had suffered particular head injuries. And we were measuring the differences in certain kinds of cognitive abilities between people whose damage was in the right hand sphere vs. the left hand sphere. There was only one person

I ever interviewed for whom his injuries were related to military service. But the others were stroke patients mostly.

I went into it for the biological question that we were pursuing but I found it very fulfilling to work with people who were trying to capture their independence back. And less heartening for the ones who did not succeed in doing so, but to be sure the ones who were working and struggling and getting somewhere, there's something very beautiful about that. And I think there's a lot of the same pleasure in children who from the earliest age are on the incline trying to capture total control of their lives, and wanting to help them do that.

Hanna: I remember, and you can correct me, that you applied to graduate school and probably got in and you were going to study—

Scott: Cognitive psychology, not biologically oriented, more the software, was what I was looking at.

Hanna: Is that related at all to your work at computers?

Scott: Absolutely. When you look at the different branches of psychology that people go into, the only people at that time who were going into cognitive psychology were computer nerds. There was a real overlap there.

Hanna: The fact that your father is a professor of psychology did not have influence with you?

Scott: Well, that's dinner table conversation. I suspect there is always some genetic overlap in terms of what interests a person. And then you add to that an environment in which so many of the people who crossed my personal life were graduate students in that department.

Hanna: Did you come here in order to support yourself? Did you look for a job?

Scott: No, no. Actually, it's funny: the thing that led to my coming here was I had had a little bit of a dry spot in consulting jobs, on computer consulting, for a variety of reasons. Not a small part of it was the tech crash back then. But between that what happened was two things. First, my work with people at Harvard had led me to a certain amount of wistfulness that I was trying to direct, that I was trying to understand. Something was missing. It didn't take me a whole lot of thinking to realize that what I found missing in the intellectual life at Harvard, was the pursuit of answers to questions and truth and all of these great things that one thinks that one's pursuing in university—the real pursuit of those things rather than what I frankly found far too often questions being asked not in order to find a real answer, but questions being asked in order to sound smart. And I found myself, I think, edging a little bit towards the depressed: Is this really what life is?

I started thinking wistfully back to the last place I had been in which there really was open intellectual honesty without any fear of being wrong, and that was this school. And that was the kids in this school and the adults in this school. And that was what I missed.

Hanna: So the thought came to your head that you wanted to be staff?

Scott: It certainly was dancing through my mind. Then I was in this period in which I had been sort of between major jobs doing computer consulting for a period of time, and something very specific happened. I got called for an interview and I debated whether or not to go, but I went. The job paid an excellent salary, something like ten times my opening salary offer from Sudbury Valley School.

I went to the interview. It was for managing computer networking for a parochial school on Long Island. I couldn't believe the amount they were paying; they didn't even have that kind of budget, but that's what the offer was. And I couldn't stand anything about the place. Then of all things, I got an offer.

Without thinking, I said no. Then I thought: I can't tell Sharon that I said no! But why the hell did I say no? I realized it was because this is too important to me. That was when I decided to talk to my friends, Mimsy and Danny, after the next Trustees' meeting, about whether they think it would be wise or unwise for me to start working at Sudbury Valley. One of the other jobs I had at that time—and this is not insignificant—was doing some public relations work for the school, just very part-time. So I was in regular contact with the school during this period. But it never quite occurred to me to think about a serious run for staff until then. After the fact, I realized that I was probably being wooed for a staff position when I was asked to do the online PR to begin with.

Hanna: So, Scott, finally you became staff. What keeps you going?

Scott: Everything. There is not a day goes by in which you don't learn something new in this job, in which you don't find three things about other people that you didn't know, in which you acquire two skills you didn't know you had it in you to get. So many things happen here of every variety. One day we're dealing with very direct physical challenges of the weather; another day we're dealing with legal complaints; another day we're trying really desperately to solve a difficult problem about how people live in the real world. In our School Meetings we're always debating, trying to figure out the right solutions in a way that lets people be themselves.

Hanna: So is it an intellectual thing only?

Scott: No, but I hope what I'm describing doesn't sound intellectual. It's not just intellectual. You're working with your gut when you're working with these questions. Obviously, you've got to use your head to make sure you're not doing something that is going to make things worse. But at the same time, to know what's important, you've got to be able to understand what others feel is important.

Hanna: Scott, I think a big motivation for people is finding a line of work that is also a meaningful use of their effort and time, which I think this school is for me. It's not about a particular skill; it's more like I'm doing it because that's my calling type of thing.

Scott: Well, I guess I agree. A calling is broader, although I don't know what it is exactly. I think that few people have only one job that would work for them, but I do think that it was very important for me to have my ultimate career—the place that I work at—be a place that is dedicated to helping people to take responsibility for themselves. That's why I could have pictured myself working at the VA hospital and helping rehabilitate people.

Every life is meaningful to someone in some way. I don't think there's any job to be done for which there isn't someone who would not feel proud and pleasure in doing it.

Hanna: I understand that, but there's a difference between pride and pleasure of problem-solving and being successful in the world than having more of a—I hate the word—a spiritual aspect to what you're doing, which satisfies more than just material or intellectual needs. But is this an idealistic job?

Scott: We get our hands too dirty for us to call this an idealistic job, I think. It's a job where you always know why you're doing what you're doing. You can hear them showing it right in the next room—the joy, the life force.

Hanna: So it fits your ideology and your everyday pleasure to see people being allowed to pursue their own selves.

Scott: Absolutely. To my mind, it's not just what I like, it's what I think is the minimum we can do for each other.

Hanna: So you are very pleased with your job here.

Scott: Absolutely.

Hanna: Do you want to add anything?

Scott: Well, there's not a person who has spent any time in this school, who's not learned from Hanna Greenberg the real value of looking for what other people have to say and digging for the gold in helping them find it.

Hanna: And you really think you learned that?

Scott: Oh, not as well as you, but I am a better person because of that. And I mean it. I think that being in contact with a person who has that skill, at the level you do, has been tremendous for everyone who has been in contact with you.

Hanna: Well, thank you Scott. You have succeeded in embarrassing me totally.

Hanna Greenberg

"You know there are a lot of things that in retrospect you don't know how you did them, but you did. I just read a book about K2, and how they came back to it after saying: I'm never going there again. It's the same thing. This school was like climbing K2."

Mimsy: This interview[1] is a part of a group of interviews that Hanna has been doing of the school's staff members. I am doing this one of her because she can't interview herself.

What are your first remembrances of thinking about child rearing and education?

Hanna: I hated school from the first grade. I did not like the way I was brought up with European-style toughness. My parents never hit us or anything, but I was constantly punished. For example, I had to finish whatever was on my plate, and I wouldn't. So I had a lot of issues with the way I was brought up. And when I met Danny, who was an American, he had similar feelings about his upbringing—different style, but issues. I guess when you're sixteen, you think about those things. And once you think about your own upbringing, you say: how am I going to raise my kids? So we did talk a lot about it.

Mimsy: What made you think you would have kids?

---

[1]This interview was done in two sections, during two different months.

Hanna: I did not want to have kids. I thought that I'd be a terrible mother because my mother was always nervous and I thought I would be nervous, so I didn't want to have kids. Danny wanted to have kids, Danny loves babies.

Mimsy: From that age?

Hanna: Always did.

Mimsy: So, as teenagers you and Danny started talking about children, about having them?

Hanna: Not about having them, but theories of child rearing.

Mimsy: And did you develop a theory that you thought was reasonable?

Hanna: No.

Mimsy: That's good because there aren't any.

Hanna: One thing had a great impact on me. We were hitching a ride with an American. Danny sat in the front so he could talk to the driver in English, and I sat in the back, and in the pocket behind the driver's seat I found a little pamphlet. So during the ride I read the beautiful story "My Little Boy", which talked about the author (who lived in Denmark) raising his child before he went to school, and how he respected his child and gave him a lot of freedom. I read it in Hebrew and I didn't remember the author's name, but I never forgot the content. Years later a student came and gave me a xerox of the story in English translation, and said: my father is sending it to you because he thinks that you would like it.

Mimsy: A student here?

Hanna: Yes. Scott Schafer. I had it reprinted. It's one of the most beautiful stories, really. It was written in the beginning of the last century, so it's about 100 years old. It's a beautiful book. I also read about Korczak, who was a Polish Jewish writer and educator, who could have escaped the Warsaw ghetto, because he was very famous, but refused. The Poles offered to save him, but he refused. He had an orphanage and he stayed with his kids and went on the train with them and perished. He wrote a lot about education and I read those books, because they were in my father's library. They're all about respect for children. So I kind of grew up with reading about those things but not getting any respect myself, not in my school and not in my house, although my parents were kind of enlightened, liberal people. So then I came to this country, I went to college, and I went to graduate school and then Michael was born.

Mimsy: Why, if you didn't want children?

Hanna: I loved children and I always babysat, it's just that I was scared. Danny said I'd be a great mother, and I knew he would be a very involved father, which had not been the case in my family. When I was eight, I had diphtheria, which is a horrible disease. Your throat constricts and people die from it. I was in bed for six months and my father came in once a day and read me a story and that was it. I missed half a year of school and I wasn't tutored and I didn't get the school's textbooks; I didn't get any help. So he wasn't involved. That's how he was. He was very involved with politics and ethics, peace.

Mimsy: Were politics, ethics and peace important to you?

Hanna: Not really. I was too young. I suffered consequences because his positions were not popular. I didn't really understand it. And I was never really a particularly political animal.

Mimsy: So you had a kid. When did you start thinking about his education?

Hanna: Michael was born in December and my birthday is in December. When he was one year old Danny gave me A. S. Neill's book, *Summerhill*, and I read it and I said: We'll go, that's what we're going to do. It really fit, because Michael is a unique individual. Everybody's unique, but he's unique in the sense that he was a very naive, "old soul", wise person, always talking and asking why. I felt that the teachers would not appreciate it and that he would be hurt, and that the beauty of his soul would be damaged, and I didn't want that done to my kid. It fit my own personal experience, but it was reinforced by Michael's personality, or the way I felt about him. I think Talya was more adaptable and savvy.

Mimsy: Girls are more adaptable.

Hanna: She would have known how to maneuver it, but I do think that she and the other girls, like your daughter and Laura Poitras, have benefited immensely from being in the school. I was the second child and I think one of the phenomena of being the second child is that the parents adapt to parenthood; they learn how to be parents with the first child. They make big decisions for the first child, and the second child just has to adapt to whatever decisions were made for the first child, unless they have big problems. If they don't, they're always adapting to whatever is decided for the first child. When we started the school, I think it was the prime time for Michael, and he was very ready, but Talya was a little bit too young. He was six, and she was just barely four. I grieve about it to this day, because I should have known better, being the second child myself, but I didn't. You can't do everything right, you just do what you can.

Mimsy: I think of it as the first child teaching the parents how to be parents and the second child getting the benefit of the trial by fire that the parents and the first child have just been through.

Hanna: That's true. I'm going to tell you a very funny story. I overheard Talya saying to Michael—I think she was six, and he was eight—"Michael, you're really stupid. You are such a goody-goody. Haven't you figured out that they love you anyway, you don't have to do what they say? You're really stupid." That's what you're talking about.

Mimsy: Exactly.

Hanna: Isn't that hilarious? But it shows exactly Michael the naive one and Talya the savvy one. She always read social cues much better than him.

Mimsy: Were you still in graduate school when Michael was born?

Hanna: Oh, absolutely. Both of them.

Mimsy: So you were extremely busy.

Hanna: Yes, but I had a lot of help. Danny was home, and I had a full-time nanny, and I had somebody clean the house. So when I came home, I felt that quality time was good. It hurt my graduate work because most of my co-workers came home and worked for hours after dinner and I did not.

Mimsy: So during these years of early childhood were you trying to figure out what was going to happen when the day came that they had to go to school?

Hanna: Children are not allowed to grow up, I thought. When you have a baby, you don't think about it. By the way, my nanny in Framingham was Margaret Parra, who was fantastic. And before that I had a very good woman in New York City. I always found very good nannies and it was an enriching experience because I was away from my country, Israel, and so I didn't have social support raising children. These people helped me enlarge the scope of my children's lives. It was very good for them actually.

Mimsy: I'm sure it was good for them. I'm sure it was good for you too. Being a mother with small children and being at home with them is a very lonely thing no matter how much social support it looks like you have.

Hanna: No, I never did that, so I don't know.

Mimsy: It's a very lonely thing. People are always sort of shocked at how lonely it is. So here your children are, growing much older, like probably three and one, or something, and you moved to Massachusetts. And you're still not thinking maybe some day they'll have to go to school? Or is Danny thinking about that?

Hanna: I don't know, I don't think so.

Mimsy: Really? You think maybe he was thinking about it and not telling you? I find that so hard to believe.

Hanna: No, I think Danny was satisfied with his own school experience. I was a terrible student, I hated school, I never did any homework. Everything I learned, I learned on my own. Danny was a very good student, and he did not really rebel against it. He only rebelled after his first year as a student at Columbia, when he left the country and reinvented himself in Israel. Until then he was okay with academia. That was the culture of his family and it was so easy for him he didn't question it. He didn't rebel. Danny creates things out of philosophical enlightenment and I do them out of rebelliousness.

Mimsy: We've never talked about this, but I've always had the feeling, because I've known you for a long time, that you were very much front and center in everything that had to do with figuring out how to make a school.

Hanna: Thank you, Mimsy, but this is a little awkward for me to talk like that. I think my strength is in feeling problems in the surrounding society, and I verbalize my concerns or my critiques, and that's about all I can do. And Danny is very good at figuring out ways to solve those problems in a practical way.

Mimsy: Well, that's what I meant.

Hanna: The JC is a good example. I said right away: if we have a school, I'm not going to be the police. I'm going to be an adult, but I'm not going to be a police. And that's probably all I could figure out. Danny was the one who figured out the judicial system.

Mimsy: But not till the school had started.

Hanna: But I would never have figured it out. I don't create systems. I break systems, I don't create them.

Mimsy: That is very interesting to me, and I'm finding it hard to believe, because I think that you're extremely creative in figuring out systems—not figuring out other people's systems, but figuring out new systems. I may have you all wrong, but I don't think I do.

Hanna: I think that the way my brain works is different than the way Danny's brain works and it just so happened that because we're together and we have so much respect for each other, it's a relationship that just happens to be creative in ways that either one alone would not be. That was not planned, it just happened. Destiny.

Mimsy: That was destiny, that's right, a very lucky happenstance.

Hanna: I do want to say one more thing. Danny and I come from very different countries, but a computer would have put us together. We have a lot in common in the way we were brought up—the religion, the philosophy, the moral underpinning of the way we were brought up are the same. So even though we're so different, the basis is common.

Mimsy: As time went on and you're getting closer to the time when Michael is going to go to school, what are you thinking about?

Hanna: We were going to find a school for him. And the first step was to write A. S. Neill at Summerhill. At that time A. S. Neill only took boarding students. So Michael's five, and I said: I was willing to move to England, but not willing to give my child to Mr. Neill. So that nixed that. I didn't even go visiting. There was ferment in this country—freedom! There were all kinds of little schools that started all over. When we visited them, we were appalled, because they were chaotic, messy, rebellious to the point of not keeping any of the good stuff of the culture; it was all, you know, "peace, love, Woodstock"-type of stuff. And we're not like that, we're really very straight.

Mimsy: Are any of those schools that you were thinking about still around?

Hanna: Not a single one.

Mimsy: Do you think they were around in 1975?

Hanna: No.

Mimsy: So they were really flashes in the pan.

Hanna: Because they really did not have coherent philosophy and they didn't develop structures. They focused so much on the rebellion part and not the building part. We were not going to have any part of it. They had drugs. They were filthy. They were loud. I didn't feel it was a conducive place for my son. And definitely not for my daughter.

Mimsy: So then what?

Hanna: So we were thinking of running away to the woods and not sending our kids to school, but at that time that was not legal or possible to do. And I did not want my kids to be lonely.

Mimsy: What does running to the woods even mean?

Hanna: It means buying a cottage in some Vermont forest.

Mimsy: And how do you make a living?

Hanna: Danny writes. It was ridiculous. I would have been lonely. It wasn't for me and it wasn't for my kid. It was a fleeting thought that was dismissed. The last thing in the world I wanted to do was start a school.

But let me go back to my story. After I got my doctorate, I got a post-doc in the Boston area. We moved from New York to Framingham, and I worked at MIT. I happened to be very meticulous, I measured everything very carefully, which was good to do for lab work in biochemistry, and I worked very hard. I had Margaret as the babysitter, Danny was at home, the kids were fine, but it was a trek from Framingham, where we lived, to go to MIT. I was really working very hard. And I published a paper. It wasn't earthshaking. When you're post-doc you kind of work for a professor and the professor suggests you have this system and you use it. I did it, and it was okay, it was good work. Six months later, three other labs published the same kind of paper, which happens all the time. They read a paper and say: let's see if it's right. And that's how they verify results and move on. I said to myself: I'm leaving my kids to do something that other people are doing anyway? I'm not doing it anymore. It all came together. It's not the only reason, but it was one of the thoughts I had that helped me leave.

While I was still working, we were starting to have meetings about the school. One day I got dressed to go to work and I said: you know, Danny, you should start looking for a property for the school. And he said, "You're telling me to do that? You go and do it." I said, "Okay, I will." I called work and I said: I'm not coming in. I called a realtor and started looking for the school. The realtor lived on Edmands Road in Framingham, and she was showing me a property across Route 9 on Salem End Road and we passed the current school property, and I said, "That's it, that's what I want." Because I grew up in Jerusalem where all the houses were built of stone, and here it's mostly all wood. I said: that's my building. And the lady, who was a Protestant, said: oh, it belongs to the Church and they never sell. And the rest is history.

Mimsy: You just passed by one thing without talking about it: the decision to start a school and then how you went about getting good people to work on it—just one small thing like that, or maybe two.

Hanna: I don't know. I think we started talking to people we knew. I know I asked Alan White's wife if she knew any people who would be interested and she gave me Joan's number. And we talked to Joan. It was networking. The League of Woman Voters helped us find some friends. This was early '60s, and we are in Massachusetts and John Kennedy got elected partly because they had held a lot of coffees!

So we did a lot of coffees. We'd ask anybody—neighbors, or anyone that we knew. Just like selling Tupperware, we were selling our idea of the school. We didn't have a name for it yet.

Mimsy: Did that make you feel funny to do that?

Hanna: I think you have to be young and dumb to undergo that kind of thing.

Mimsy: I think so too. It sounds horrible.

Hanna: Yes, it was. You know there are a lot of things that in retrospect you don't know how you did them, but you did. I just read a book about K2, and how they came back to it after saying: I'm never going there again. It's the same thing. This school was like climbing K2.

Mimsy: This school is still like climbing K2 sometimes. So you're sort of trying to figure out ways to network by this time.

Hanna: We wrote a lot of letters.

Mimsy: Who was "we" beside you and Danny?

Hanna: Priscilla Paris helped us. Danny had some books that he wanted typed and she was a typist and then we became friends and then she helped us. I think we really did it mostly alone in the beginning. These were very difficult years. You can only do it when you're young and idealistic and wanting it so badly for your own children. I wouldn't have done it for myself.

Mimsy: I don't understand now how people do it. From the very beginning of other people saying, "How could I do this?" my answer is always: move to Massachusetts, you don't want to do this. And some people have. But most of them have tried instead. And some have succeeded, but not without tremendous difficulties.

Hanna: I think that what really hurt was that both Danny and I considered ourselves to be articulate, and we very quickly found that the way we explain things or use certain words were not the way people heard them, which was a new phenomenon to me because in the science world people may disagree with your solutions or conclusions, but we talk the same language—it's more defined. But when you talk about things like freedom and responsibility and child rearing, it's so laden with emotion and with the personal history of each individual, and with the nuances of their understanding, that you don't communicate properly. I felt betrayed, and I wasn't used to that. I came from a world of science and not of psychology, and I was not prepared for people's emotional responses. I don't have a nice way to say it, but I wasn't prepared for the extent to which people's subconscious overwhelmed their conscious intercourse with me. I always felt that I'm not talking to a person in the same language—the subterranean language is constantly erupting like a volcano. And I wasn't prepared for it, psychologically, at all. It took a terrible toll. And it took a huge toll on Danny. Danny was very nervous those years. We were both very nervous because we started the school; we saw the building, it was for sale by the time we got organized, and we bought it for $80,000. We had saved a lot of money in order to go to Israel, because when you go to Israel you have to buy an apartment, you can't just rent.

Mimsy: You were planning to move to Israel?

Hanna: Yes. And you have to buy your refrigerator, and all that stuff, so you need start-up money. We had that money, so we put it into the school. But it was scary; we were middle-class, but we didn't have a lot of money. To put down $40,000 on this venture—$20,000 down payment on the building, and the other $20,000 to start the school—was really scary. We had a house, we had our own cars, so we felt that we could do it. Danny was always very comfortable in his ability to earn money, so he never had anxieties about his own family having enough. But he had anxieties about the school having enough money. Very quickly, during the first year after a few months, the school took over the mortgage and that was off our shoulders; that was wonderful.

We started the school with almost no money, it's amazing. This building was such a white elephant that nobody wanted it. It was like junk—it's hard to believe about this gorgeous, gorgeous property.

Mimsy: Life was not the same then as it is now—where if you see a building, you have to buy it sort of that minute, or somebody else will.

Hanna: I don't know. This building is even big for people who want a big house.

Mimsy: So after the school started, how did you feel about the school?

Hanna: I want to say that before the school started, we produced some literature about it and we really networked everywhere. So a lot of people came for interviews and I did . . . maybe 150 interviews in the house, in my living room. So a lot of people came. It was a time of turmoil in this country, and people were open to trying new things. They were very clear that they didn't like what was going on. The solutions were varied, not only with what we were doing, but there was this ferment and seeking. It was a very good time to start the school.

Mimsy: I guess in that sense it was. In fact, maybe the only time, maybe that was another piece of kismet.

Hanna: The other thing that was really disappointing was this: We were always very "square"; we were educated, we went to college and graduate school, we were not hippies, and we didn't use drugs. So we were considered "square". The only place where we were "far out", as they used to say in those days, was educating our children, and the school. The people who I thought would love the school were people talking about freedom, marching on the street under the slogan "peace, love, Woodstock". And it turned out that they didn't want freedom for their kids. They rebelled against their parents, and once they settled down into parenthood, they became like their parents with the job with big money, and the sleek cars. Earlier, they had just been kids in college having fun marching around.

Mimsy: Have you ever marched anywhere for anything?

Hanna: Never. My father came from Germany and from a very young age, I remember him saying, "If you see a lot of people marching, they're not serious, they're being used." Because he saw the Nazis come to power, and he said that people marching are scary. I was raised like that. The only time Danny went on a march, he went to Martin Luther King's Million Man March on Washington, and actually met his father there even though they didn't know that each of them was going. That was interesting because Danny is not politically active—ever. But it was a beautiful experience for him, a beautiful speech. You can identify with it, every word he said was beautiful. He was a real visionary.

Mimsy: So the school opens. How did it feel in the first weeks, besides being tired?

Hanna: Exhausting. We started in the summer, July 1st, 1968. I remember the dress I wore, and I remember the first day I didn't eat or drink and at 5 o'clock I went and drank a lot of water and I realized that I was not listening to my own body, I was only working. It was really tough. It was tough because it was very hard on Talya and I was so focused on doing the school, I was not good to her. I really feel awful about it. Do you feel like that about Debra?

Mimsy: No. I feel that way about Seth, in a different way. Even though I was with him a lot when he was little—I didn't work full-time—I have nightmares, and in them, there's a baby and I know it's mine and it's maybe a year old and I'm clear that I've never fed it or changed its diaper or anything. It's just plain neglect.

Anyway, that's not what we're talking about. So that was the first day of school. Was there any respite after that? I know there were staff meetings ever single evening.

Hanna: Yes, it was incredible work. It was creating a new world, and we were strangers in the world that we were creating. I'm Israeli, and Israel was a country that was basically built in the 1920s. I was born in 1935, and then you had all those refugees coming from Europe and the Middle East, and one of the things that a founder of the country said was, "If you want it, you can do it! If you want it, it doesn't have to be a legend. You can make it real." This is how we grew up in Israel. So I wanted a school. I was married to a guy who could do it; let's do it! I think also that being Israeli, I come from a place where they built a country, where they opened their doors to all refugees even though they had no money. From 1945 to 1948, the British closed the borders of Israel to refugees from Europe, because the Arab population didn't want them. So there was illegal immigration. The Israelis would buy rickety boats in Europe and stuff them with refugees under very difficult conditions, and then try to reach the border.

The Israelis would go to the beach with clothes, and if the boat was not intercepted they would have row boats and they would get the refugees, put them on the beach, immediately change their clothes to Israeli clothes, and take them home. There was a huge illegal immigration, and that's what I grew up with. We did what we had to do. We had very little money; my family lived in a very small house and we took in a young woman refugee in 1935, when I was born, and she lived on a fold-up camp bed in the tiny room that my brother and I shared. She lived there for six years. That's how we all grew up. I had cousins who lived in a room without electricity and the way they made money was taking in laundry; she ironed the shirts in our tiny hall. We had a refrigerator, and two of our neighbors had keys to the house so that they could put their butter and milk in our refrigerator, that was half the size of an American refrigerator. It's wonderful to grow up like that, it really is. It gives you courage to do anything.

Mimsy: Yes, it makes you very strong.

Hanna: We felt rich, you understand? We had our own house, we had the refrigerator because my mother loved gadgets.

Mimsy: There were many waves of immigrants in my house when I was a young child.

Hanna: So you know what I'm talking about. And you were not rich either, but you fed them.

Mimsy: We weren't rich, but it never occurred to me that we were poor, at that time. We weren't. We were fine. We had food. Everybody had clothes. And we had a nice apartment, an apartment that was big enough to stretch for three or four or five people for a few months. It was what you were supposed to do.

So the school got going in the summer, but not really. Do you have any memories of that time?

Hanna: Well, the kids had a wonderful time.

Mimsy: Were they terrorized by anybody?

Hanna: Probably, yes. We accepted anyone who doesn't look insane in the enrollment interview, and we still do. And sometimes people have anger, and we all know that often people who have been oppressed, when they have the opportunity, will oppress somebody weaker than them. I know that our boys had to deal with that.

Mimsy: Do you think little kids have to deal with that now?

Hanna: I don't know, maybe some. Not as much. I think it reflected the temper of the times. A lot of those kids were here because they were hippies; they were in rebellion mode and they were angry and they were using a lot of drugs. I think that sometimes if they were mad at the staff, they took it out on the staff kids. It caused me horrible pain, not relative to Talya, but for Michael.

Mimsy: What were your biggest worries that summer?

Hanna: I don't know. I think the biggest worry was the safety of the kids in the school, and teaching the parents and the kids the philosophy. I still worry about that with every little kid. I don't think that the enrollment interview and the literature, which we have in abundance, make you understand it, until you experience it. And to a certain extent, we didn't understand it either. So we had this dream, we had this vision, and most of the vision came about by saying, "We will *not* . . . !" Everything was negative— no coercion, no policing the kids, everything was a reaction to what we didn't like in our upbringing and in our schools. It took time to create a positive environment. So we had this dream, and I have to say that it's a very rare gift that I was given, that the reality of the dream has turned out to be better than the fantasy. That the school is more wondrous and beautiful and ethical and amazing than I could ever have imagined, because I never experienced it myself. Even in my dreams I could not conjure up such a beautiful thing.

Yesterday I did an interview with "Laughbox", who is sixteen, during which he says, "You know, I'm not as outgoing as Elise. She's such a friendly person, I wish I was like her." Elise is six years old. I thought: oh my God, what a beautiful place we've created, where teenagers are aware of the characters of the little kids! Because when I was a kid, nobody existed except my friends. Not older people, not adults, nobody—just my friends, my peer group. And I didn't even think of my parents as people. Here I see kids talk about their parents with great concern. They talk about siblings. They talk about other people's children.

Mimsy: I always feel that there was a point when I realized that I was learning *values* from the student body—not from one student necessarily, but from the way the student body was, and the expectations the student body had on itself and on each other. It's not that it's perfect here.

Hanna: What do you mean by values?

Mimsy: Things like levels of kindness, and the ability to let people be themselves.

Hanna: We even didn't have the vocabulary to express what happens here on a daily basis.

Mimsy: And the kids did. After a while I began to realize things like: what do I do when I see a bug? I kill it. What do I do when a child sees a bug?

Hanna: You let it go.

Mimsy: Some of the times, they're really little things. But they have to do with respect for life.

Hanna: Reverence for life. And those kids have it.

Mimsy: So that's caused me to rethink a lot of things and to be a lot more tolerant towards my fellow man, in general, as long as it's not a particular fellow man.

Hanna: Those kids are raised better than we were raised.

Mimsy: But they also teach each other by osmosis, and their values get stronger here—a lot stronger.

Hanna: That's like the article that Michael wrote a long time ago about soccer, where he talks about the way older kids treated little children. I didn't even realize how beautiful it was until now. Again, because I didn't have the eyes to see it. It's going on with basketball every day.

Mimsy: That's right. It's not unnatural. It's just the way it happens.

Hanna: All of them are like that. That's the culture. We were able to create a culture, and what I'm saying is that the fantasy was short of the reality because we couldn't even dream of doing what is happening here.

Mimsy: And that's also something we can never get across to strangers or parents.

Hanna: I think the way the kids do the JC is mind-boggling. So when the school created the judicial system, I don't think that we ever sat down and said, "The judicial system is the heart of the school that takes care of interpersonal relationships, and the integrity of the building, and the property of each individual." But any time a kid does something that is destructive to property, the JC sits there and listens, finds out what's going on, and thinks up a sentence. I sit there once every ten days, and yes I say things, but it's really the clerks who run it, every day at 11:00, and most members are there every day at 11:00—whether you are a little six-year-old or a teenager—and they come and they sit there for as long as the meeting takes—sometimes hours. Nobody who designed it could have imagined how it would work.

Mimsy: In other Sudbury schools, they often use the youngest child as the runner, partly because they don't think the youngest child can concentrate enough.

So, I want to go back to the fall of 1968. You were talking about the nasty atmosphere with some of the kids who were here.

Hanna: First of all, we had about 120 kids, which is probably too big a group to start an institution like this. We had staff who were not experienced. We kind of accepted anybody who wanted to be staff.

Mimsy: Hanna's theory of self-elimination.

Hanna: And we didn't really have a lawbook or a JC or systems to deal with the problems that arose. Every night I would do all the trash when I closed the school. We did everything. We had no money. We were young. I was 32, I was full of energy. I think we very quickly got into a severe crisis because, as I said, the hippies who had settled down to jobs and parenthood and buying a house, turned out to want a school for their children like they had when they went to school. So all of the yearning for freedom expressed itself in drugs and music and sexual liberty and not in child rearing. They thought I was very square and weird because I didn't buy into their philosophy. I don't want to come across as if I think I'm better than them, I just think we're very different. We thought that we could converge and we didn't. So very quickly, they wanted us to have classes for their kids, they wanted more of a dress code.

In late October, those parents organized and they felt more than justified in taking over the school because they said this was a democracy and they were organizing a takeover. They felt morally justified to take away the building from us, even though we were the ones who bought it. There was a huge meeting and it was like a lynch mob. And the people who protected us were the teenagers here, because they had tasted freedom and respect and they were beginning to understand. Even if they maybe brought drugs to school and did all kinds of stuff that really is not acceptable, they knew that they got respect. And that meant a lot to them.

We had a friend who was the minister of the Congregational Church, and he gave me his card and said, "Call me tomorrow." I didn't sleep all night. I was crying all night. I called him in the morning and he said, "Get rid of them." I said: how? And he said: offer them the money back. Well, the money was $350. I said: they have money. He said: trust me, I know people better than you—you're a scientist, you don't know, even well-off people will use it as an excuse to withdraw. So we offered them the money, and half of them took it and left. And it purified the school, it got rid of the venom, the entitlement, the negativity, the viciousness. And then we could start building the school.

I must relate one of my contributions—and I will show off a little now. When we moved in 1968 from Framingham to Sudbury it was an election year, and I wanted to vote in the primary. I was registered in Framingham and I came to Sudbury and they said: you're not registered here. And I said: I'm registered in Framingham. And they said: "No, you have to register in your own town and you have to be here three months. You haven't lived here for three months." So I insisted when we drafted the by-laws that nobody would have a vote in Sudbury Valley's ruling body (the "Assembly" of the original bylaws, in which parents had a vote) until they are here for three months. October was not three months, and they didn't have the vote. I am very proud of that. If that didn't happen to me, they would have taken it away from us.

Mimsy: That's wonderful. How 'bout that!

Hanna: How could you anticipate that? I just was thinking a lot about it at the time. It's reasonable for a parent to say, "Okay, I put my money down, I'm sending my kids and I really don't like the way the school is. I'll leave. I don't want to take it away from the people who worked on it. I know it's not mine—just because I paid some tuition.

Mimsy: But they felt that it's a democracy, everybody's equal.

Hanna: Well, obviously, they were mistaken, the whole "Assembly" idea was a mistake. It took us forty-five years to correct it. But theoretically, it was beautiful, yes? We are living in America, we tried to make a democracy here at the school, and we didn't realize that it has to be a democracy of people who have a stake of "residence" in the community.

Mimsy: It was not an easy thing to realize, really.

Hanna: Then the school really settled. We slowly worked on the furniture, we worked on the books, and there was a lot of talking to kids, talking to parents, talking to each other, refining our everyday behavior according to the experience that we were gaining. In the meantime, our kids were having a blast because they were just playing like at recess or at summer vacation. And they were blossoming. The kids were doing great.

Mimsy: And they could play in the evening anywhere they wanted because there were no restrictions, because we were here in the evening. In the beginning we had meetings all the time.

* * * * *

Hanna: When we started the school, we were thirty, our kids were 4 and 6. Then each of our families had another child, David and Seth.

Mimsy: We did. Actually, not together but separately, but almost together.

Hanna: Those boys are 46 now. They left school when they were about 18, and we're still here. We're still working very hard. We're still very emotionally involved with the welfare of the school. We said, as did Mikel Matisoo and Joan Rubin, that as soon as our kids graduate, we are going to be out of here. Well, we're not out of here. And that says to me that it's a very meaningful way to spend your life. Even if we started because of our children, it certainly evolved into caring about all children.

Mimsy: Today I've been going through all of the staff interviews trying to get them together as something that has some flow. And basically, everyone says, in one way or another, this is great work. But I also think we—you and I—work much harder than we did when our children were here. I think we have more time. And we've chosen to put a lot of that time into the school.

Hanna: That's true about you. I don't know if it's true about me.

Mimsy: Well, you had an interruption in your flow of life.

Hanna: The car accident, when I was very severely injured; my son David was fifteen. That was a terrible thing. I used to think about it almost every day. It took me twenty years to adapt, adjust, accept this useless, totally pointless accident. I had my son David in my car, as well as two other staff members, David Gould and Marj Wilson, because we were going on our fall hiking trip. That was a big blow and that did set me back.

Mimsy: I don't know if you ever realized how many years you improved and improved and improved. You're amazing.

Hanna: I remember vividly that a doctor said: this healing will take you a long time, don't ever look at a clock, it's going to be at least five years before you feel that you have overcome the deficit. And I said to myself: great, I'll be senile before I heal, that's really great.

Mimsy: Luckily, you aren't.

Hanna: One thing that happens in the brain is that you create new neural pathways constantly, and it does take a long time. But I did a lot of therapy and I had a lot of exercises. One of them was to write, so first of all, I learned how to type. My daughter, Talya, who is a therapist, said: "You have a whole year that you can't go to work, you might as well find a way to use it constructively to learn something, otherwise, you will be miserable." And she gave me a book about learning how to write, because I always complained that I can't write. The name of the book was *Writing on Both Sides of the Brain*. It was very helpful, and I did learn how to write. I always laugh, Mimsy, that you're a good writer because you can just sit down and write or that's how it looks to me, whereas with me, it's a painful process—not pleasant. Sometimes I just have to write something because I have something I want to say, but I'd rather not.

Mimsy: Well I think it's very interesting that you are a good writer now. The school to me is a place where one continues to grow. And who can ask for more than that?

Hanna: We always had a lot of strife between parents and us. It was very painful to me because I always put a lot of my effort into explaining the school and the philosophy and trying to draw them in and alleviate their anxieties, and one of the things that one parent said to me, which really stung, is "this school is more for you than for the kids, because you're learning a lot of things; the staff is using the school to grow."

Mimsy: I would hope so.

Hanna: And I was thinking to myself: you want us to stand still and stagnate? I didn't answer, I don't answer those kinds of things. It really stung. I thought a lot about it, over the years. In fifty years there has been a lot of change in our culture. If we were the kind of people who didn't grow and stay current with the times, we couldn't work here. It is true of everyone on the staff. We're very curious people, we know what's going on around the world-at-large, as well as our little world. We talk a lot among ourselves about how to improve whatever we're doing. We're not sitting on our laurels.

Mimsy: We don't have any laurels.

Hanna: Yes, we do. Our alumni are really exceptional people. They are kind, they're generous, they work hard at whatever they want to do, they keep learning new things. They are leading very exceptional lives each in their own way, they are very different and they are remarkable people. As we started this interview, I said I did it for my kids. And I can look back and say, "Well, what you wanted to do, you did. You gave your kids and other people's children—thousands of them—the space, the time, the respect, the support to become the best selves that they possibly could become." So, I do think that's very, very rewarding.

We have two kinds of kids here. We have kids who come when they are little kids because their parents really like the philosophy. And they stay here ten years, twelve years, and they're all remarkable people in their own way. And then we have kids who come because they had trouble adjusting to public school. Usually, they're creative, they are too active to sit still, they are very curious kids. A lot of them come when they're older and after a year of adjusting, also find themselves. They are the kids who are more grateful to us, ironically. They're the ones who say Sudbury Valley saved my life, and their parents say the same thing. We didn't save their life, what we saved was their selves. I remember one girl said to me: when I was six, I knew who I was, and then I lost it; and then I came here and I found myself again. That was a beautiful thing.

The more I see public schools and private schools, the more I see of the educational system, the more critical I am of it, because now I have confidence that what we are doing creates kids who are knowledgeable, who are capable of going out to the world and succeeding in whatever pursuit they decide—whether it's medicine, computers, childcare, marriage, whatever they want to do. And they do not need to lose their selves.

Mimsy: I knew that they got a tremendous amount here but I never used to say they got a great education. I didn't put it together that way. It *is* a great education. The kids who leave here know a tremendous amount—whether or not it's the same stuff that other people know is not important. They know how to find everything out, so it doesn't matter at all whether it's the same stuff other people know. But they are very well educated in general.

Hanna: My favorite thing that I think about is you have a kid who's six and doesn't read yet. They go to public school, or any traditional school, and are taught how to read. Well, middle class families like us and have kids who come here, they read to their kids all the time. So some kids learn how to read and others don't—they didn't figure out how to crack the code. To force them to read does not leave a good taste in their mouth about reading. And it doesn't give them the feeling of triumph. If you wait until the kid is ready, even if they're nine or ten, then reading is a great discovery of a tool that will be enjoyable to you for the rest of your life.

Mimsy: I have a theory about that. I think the kids who read early, in general, take in less of the nuance of the world around them, and the kids who read later are so busy doing that they can't stop. It's not 100% true, sometimes kids are doing things both ways.

Hanna: They read the world, they don't read stories.

Mimsy: One of the things I have enjoyed seeing this year is kids giving each other the space and time to practice reading, when playing games where you have to read stuff. You almost always have to read stuff with board games. Trivia is full of big words, but there's other stuff that's full of not quite so big words. And you know, just waiting, quietly and patiently, while the kids figure out the words, or spell out a word to ask for help if they need. It is so beautiful to see. It is the golden rules, really: they treat the kids that know less exactly as they would want to be treated in those circumstances.

Hanna: Or in the JC, they will wait until the clerk writes ever so slowly when they can write faster.

Mimsy: Oh my gosh, yes. It's very hard for me to do that sometimes, as an adult, very hard—especially, if it's a long report.

Hanna: So what keeps us going here? It's interesting, it's meaningful, it's enjoyable most of the time. It's also heartbreaking. It is ironic that this country that is by far the freest society on earth is less free with their children than people in so-called primitive societies where kids are allowed to learn by observation and participation and have to learn really life-saving skills. For instance, the Kalahari people: they have to learn to track, they have to learn what foods are safe and which are not. There's a lot of knowledge just to survive there in very harsh conditions. And I guess if you measure the number of facts they have to take in, compared to what they learn here, they probably learn just as much—human capacity to learn is always there. And our society doesn't let kids do that.

I also happen to think that it's harder to get new enrollees now than it was twenty or so years ago.

Mimsy: No question. I think that people have grown accustomed to thinking that standardized tests like MCAS are okay—they're just the way it is—while at first people were horrified by the fact that their kids would be taught merely material on tests. Now they don't even think about it, it seems. And people do buy into having their children do homework. There's no question that having your children do homework is one of the ways you can relate to your children because you maybe nag them, you help them, you have to make sure they finish it—it sounds so awful. And you know what they are doing while they are doing it!

Hanna: But it's negative relating.

Mimsy: Negative is right.

Hanna: Parents tell us when they come here that they are so relieved because it was a negative experience. The kids are angry at the parents for coercing them, they're not feeling that they are helped or that they are relating to parents, they feel coerced, they feel angry.

Mimsy: But they also are in a situation where they're just doing what everybody else does and it doesn't seem strange to them. It's horrible.

Hanna: You're saying that they're not questioning it.

Mimsy: They're not questioning it. The parents are not questioning it and the children are not questioning it. And I don't know why. But the kind of bureaucracy and just the sheer power of the schooling system and its many, many tentacles are pretty amazing to me. It has to change and I thought that it would have toppled by now. In 1968 I assumed that in fifty years, or even thirty years, public education would have collapsed. It was too cumbersome to keep going. And I was wrong, completely wrong. It's just gotten stronger. People used to ask whether I could picture our school at the age of 25. I would say that the world of education would be so much different that I didn't know if we would still be needed. Ha!

Hanna: I always found it so sad, coming from an economically third-world country, where there was a very great value placed on education; it was like a little European country. There were very highly educated people and also many not educated. I used to think the Marxist thing; that if you give people food and shelter that they'll be happy.

Mimsy: Why?

Hanna: Because suffering, hunger and want is very stressful. And I see people here in the suburbs of Boston where they're quite well off—with big houses, big yards, big modern schools—and everybody's stressed. You would think they have arrived at the American success story. And they're not relaxing, they're stressed.

Mimsy: Well, they have to keep pedaling all the time. They don't get to stop.

Hanna: They're like the mouse on the wheel. They are stressed about their kids: how are they going to get into a "good college"?

Mimsy: They're stressed by their life, by their values. Their values stress them.

Hanna: Is it really important to get into a good college? It's ridiculous, it really is ridiculous.

Mimsy: Yes, it is. And we see that here too because we now see a lot of kids who are getting college tutoring, not just in subjects, but even getting someone to help them figure out what kind of college to go to. Since when do they need that?

Hanna: It's all a myth. We talked about what kept us going because, you know the Jewish saying: whoever saves one person, is like one who saves the whole world.

Mimsy: There's a second thing. I know you know it. I said I didn't used to talk about SVS alums as having gotten a good education. It wasn't that I didn't think it, but somehow those weren't the words. We have more words now, and that is also keeping you here.

Hanna: I went to graduate school in a very prestigious university. But everything I am doing, everything that I know, I studied on my own. It's not from what I learned in the university. The same thing in true of my high school and then college—what I'm doing is totally different from anything I was taught.

I know students who are older say that one year here has given them a different way to look at the world, which is independent and critical. It's amazing because we don't preach, we don't teach, we just let them be. Everybody wants to pass on their culture and their knowledge to the young. That's a very natural thing.

Mimsy: Well, we're very American, we're like 1000% American and we have our judicial system which is a really important tool for every person's ability to get along here—they know it, and they understand their power in it, and they understand the values. And those are not subliminal, those are right up front. We're not giving them lectures, but we don't need to. The ability to interact with people of every age extends the culture naturally to the young.

Hanna: You're talking like a literary person, but I am a science person.

Mimsy: I am a literary person.

Hanna: I like facts. And I don't share some of the facts that I enjoy learning about.

Mimsy: Oh, I see, you mean you don't share with everybody what you wish you did?

Hanna: It's a natural thing to talk about what you know and what you care about. But here, you're only able to do it if people really ask you.

Mimsy: Sometimes. Sometimes you read a book or see a movie, and it's fun or fascinating, or deep, and you know somebody that would be interested. So you tell people about it.

Hanna: What I'm trying to say is that sometimes the natural inclination to pass on the culture to the young is not satisfied here because the young that happen to be here are not at the same page at the time that you want to talk about those things.

Mimsy: That's right, that's exactly right. Annoying, isn't it?

Hanna: That's frustrating to teacher-types.

Mimsy: I'm not a teacher-type.

Hanna: I think all adults are teachers because you teach your kids how to live. You teach them how to tie their shoes, or say thank you.

However, to change the subject, one of the wonderful things about coming here is you walk in the school and students of all ages greet you. And they're busy and sometimes they are too busy to say hello but often they do. That's very heartwarming. And the little girls always greet you with great glee and warmth and kindness—the boys are too busy. You come to work and you get this beautiful warmth from young people, and you know that you are making a difference in their lives.

Mimsy: Yes, you're also extending the number of years in which you have contact with something that keeps you much younger.

Dionne Ekendiz

"It's really hard . . . to run a Sudbury school and to hold the philosophy that kids are capable of educating themselves and solving their own problems and handling their own conflicts. A lot of adults think it's neglect when you don't try to guide children or be involved in their issues from day to day . . . I think I had more respect for the kids and more confidence in their skills."

Hanna: Dionne, can you just tell us a little bit about yourself?

Dionne: I grew up in Florida, in a predominantly Hispanic community and then I came to university in Boston.

Hanna: You are partially Cuban, right?

Dionne: Yes, my mother is Cuban.

Hanna: When I talk to you, you always say that when you're with Hispanics they're more fun, they're alive—I hear nostalgia.

Dionne: Yeah, of course. But it's funny, because when I'm with them I poke fun at them for being so in my business. Why do you always scream, can't you talk like a normal person? I guess I didn't really consider south Florida to be necessarily home. Whenever I am down there I feel more American, because my father's American. And I think differently than most people down there.

Hanna: When you were a kid did you like school?

Dionne: Up to a certain point. When I stopped liking school, I remember thinking this is a game, this school thing, these grade things, and I knew how to play it well. So I could get good grades without really doing that much work. And then getting into college was another game. I had to get a really good score on the SATs so I studied for that, and I had to have a really good GPA; and it helps to be well-rounded. I liked sports so that was a genuine interest of mine. I played sports and I was involved in clubs. It was a formula.

Hanna: And you went to MIT.

Dionne: Because I got accepted to MIT and I felt like I had to go if I got accepted. I think that was the only one I applied to actually. So it was either that or community college or literally work at the supermarket.

Hanna: Do you like the fact that MIT was prestigious?

Dionne: My parents really liked it—they got to brag. But I thought, if I was playing a game, I might as well win.

Hanna: Did you know what you wanted to study at MIT?

Dionne: Not really, but I knew I was good at math.

Hanna: Was it a good place for you?

Dionne: It's the only college experience I know. I made the most of it. I played sports—soccer, basketball and softball. The last year I lived in an apartment, in Boston, with a roommate, a Puerto Rican girl. We had a lively apartment that year.

Hanna: After you graduated from MIT, what did you do?

Dionne: I went to work at Ford, in Michigan. I did a summer internship, the summer after junior year. All the companies came and recruited at the time, which was the early '90s. And I said well, that was a good experience, I'll go back and try again.

Hanna: How was Michigan?

Dionne: There was beautiful parts of it. I love new places and I love new experiences, and I can find the good in everything. But I didn't really like living and working there. The environment was an automobile manufacturing plant. I stayed about a year and a half. But I had a really good friend who I actually played soccer with at MIT, and she was working at Microsoft in Seattle. We talked a lot. She said come live with me, I have a two-bedroom apartment. Just pack up your things. The very next day I handed in my two-week resignation. My boss thought I was joking.

I was on the fast-track to management plan; that meant you were already chosen to be the leader there one day—I don't know, vice-president or something. And then I moved out to Seattle. I moved in with my friend, and I was much happier.

Hanna: What did you do in Seattle?

Dionne: I enjoyed it, I had a good time. I worked at Microsoft for a year, I was just a software tester. It was fun: it's a completely different culture from Ford which is an old company.

Hanna: Are you good at computers?

Dionne: I'm okay, I wouldn't call myself a computer geek but I pick up whatever I need to learn pretty quickly. There are people that like computers and they learn about them just for the sake of knowing more, and I use computers as a tool. So I learn when I need something, when I need to use it as a tool to achieve some goal. So Microsoft wasn't a place for me, because I really wasn't that interested in computers. And I thought well let me try this engineering thing again and so I went to Boeing, in Seattle, and I got on airplanes.

Hanna: Having been to MIT opens doors for you in these companies, doesn't it?

Dionne: Yeah, it does, I have to admit. But you know at a certain point, it's kind of insulting to go to an interview and the person hiring really doesn't ask you any questions to challenge you or anything. They just see your resume and they say oh, MIT, this is a no-brainer. And you get a little checkbox. I know it sounds really bratty of me, or ungrateful, to say something like that.

Hanna: But they're going by statistics, and statistically speaking it's hard to get into MIT and the kids there are competent and they know what they want to study. I worked there you know. It's a very highly thought of place. So it works for them, the recruiters, statistically.

Then you got married.

Dionne: I got married and we wanted to have kids. I had met him when I was an undergrad. He was a sailor, so he would go off on the ships for two months and come home for a month and basically come to wherever I was for about three years. And then after three years I told him, every time you leave you're taking a risk. And he said give me two months and he quit his job and he settled in Seattle as well. So I guess we were serious. That was 24 years ago.

Hanna: Did you always imagine you would have kids?

Dionne: I don't think I ever questioned it.

Hanna: Did you and he discuss child-rearing when you were dating?

Dionne: No, not at all. I think I took it for granted that I would be the decision-maker when it came to child-rearing. But I observed him. We were together I think twelve years before we had children. I knew he was a good person, he was honest, he was honorable.

Hanna: I understand that, but did he know that about you?

Dionne: No, he liked a little spice. I knew he would be a good dad so we didn't talk about child-rearing.

Hanna: When did you think of schooling?

Dionne: I didn't like this whole engineering path that I was on—computer science engineering—it wasn't personally fulfilling for me. But it paid the bills, it paid well, and it was somewhat easy for me. I always knew I wanted to work with kids and be some sort of a teacher. I've always coached and tutored kids, and I've always been around kids. So I said okay, I'm pregnant now and it would be nice to walk hand-in-hand with my children to the local public elementary school right around the corner. So I went and got my Master's in education and while I was there, I did some research on the local public schools—the best public schools in Broward County, Ft. Lauderdale area. I saw a lot of really messed up things.

Hanna: That was before your own kids went to school.

Dionne: I was pregnant at the time. And I realized all these things I was willing to do to other people's kids, I was not willing to do to my children. It was a wake-up call for me. I can't do this. And then I started researching—researching different educational philosophies—you know, the big ones: Montessori, Waldorf, etc. And I found Sudbury Valley by chance online, and immediately I was attracted. After my first child was born, I spent lots of time on the couch while she napped or nursed. And I read a lot of the Sudbury Valley books.

It was a no-brainer for me. I started asking my husband if we could move to Massachusetts. It took him ten years to agree, but here we are. Because he wouldn't move! I also tried to get him to move to other Sudbury schools. I wasn't crazy enough to open a school. I just wanted my children to go to one. So I said let's go back to Seattle, because there's one there. And he said no, no, no, that's too far away, we've done that. You know, I gave him a couple of options. It wasn't going to happen; he wanted to stay put for a while.

He had a job he enjoyed. I was willing to compromise. So I said okay, I have to open a Sudbury school here. And somehow he agreed.

Hanna: How old was your daughter?

Dionne: Well, we started when she was two, planning, meeting, etc. And then the school opened when she was four. We opened the school with nine children. My youngest child was one, and my mom and my husband babysat her two days a week and I would take her to the school three days a week.

The nine kids became a family. With nine kids, you have to. This was 2010. I worked there for six years.

At some point, in the fifth year, we were up to like 25 students and it started feeling like a real school. I always thought forty would be a target. Anyway, that only lasted a couple months. By Christmas we were down to 15 students again. People moved back to where they came from. Maybe one family got divorced and the father wasn't willing to pay for the school anymore. There were different reasons, nothing to do with the school itself.

After feeling like we had arrived—the 25 students—and feeling the energy of the school and feeling like this is what I pictured, to drop so suddenly within three or four months felt like starting at the beginning again and I think I was crushed, that it was too hard. And then I thought about my own daughters. That's the reason I started it, so they can experience this type of schooling. And I thought the school is not going to be big enough for them. I know in a few years, when they become pre-teens or teens, they're going to need more peers. They're going to ask if they can go to another school. And I would let them. So I thought what am I doing this for. I was done. So I really started working on my husband to move up here. And he said okay; in two years. He finally agreed.

Hanna: Were you invited here to be on Diploma Committees?

Dionne: Twice. I loved it. Everyone was thanking me—all of you Sudbury staff—for putting in all this work. And I was like, why are you thanking me? It was such a wonderful experience for me, I felt like it was a gift. The kids who were trying to graduate were amazing, and most of them don't know how amazing they are.

Hanna: What do you mean by that?

Dionne: They were really self-aware, they were comfortable in their own skin for the most part. I'm not going to say all of them were. They had all come in at different places in their lives. But, in general, I just remember being so impressed by the quality of person that left here.

Hanna: So that strengthened your belief that that's what you want to do for your kids?

Dionne: I would say it definitely strengthened it. I was already convinced before.

Hanna: Were your parents supportive of the way you were bringing up your daughters, and starting a school?

Dionne: They were nervous. They were really hands-off parents. And I thank them for it because really they trusted me. I was a fairly good kid, I stayed out of trouble, or I didn't tell them the things I did. They were nervous for my daughters. They thought that they should follow the same path I did because it worked for me, so why wasn't I allowing my daughters to follow that same path? They were nervous but they didn't fight me.

But there came a point where three or four years into the school, I think when my first daughter started reading, at about seven or eight, that they just completely relaxed and they were like okay, Dionne was right, this can happen on its own, this learning process. And then they know the girls and they know how smart they are and funny and loving, what else do you want for your grandkids? And happy!

Hanna: So for you, hating public school was not a motivator to start your own school.

Dionne: That's hard for a lot of people to understand. They say, "Why are you doing this thing so contradictory to traditional education when traditional education obviously worked for you?" It's hard for them to understand that actually it was a process of de-schooling myself. As I said, school was a game that I was good at, and I learned not to work hard, I was on the treadmill and I didn't really know what I wanted. I stayed on the treadmill and I was getting awards. So later I became a typical recovering "A" student.

The critiques did not come from friends. They were really supportive of me and what I was doing, and the fact that I opened the school. Some of them came to visit. A lot of them came to help, like painting the school or donating stuff.

Hanna: Were you depressed as a high school kid?

Dionne: No, I wasn't depressed because I had a lot of freedom outside of school. I had a job and I had a car. And because I was such a good student, if I ever left school there must be a good reason. So I had a lot of freedom. But looking back, it's a little depressing because I wasted so much time. School was a waste of time. And even at MIT, to some extent I wasted a lot of time there, because I was just trying to graduate, get that piece of paper, and not really studying what I liked, or even knowing what I really liked. I was just on the treadmill, a leaf in the wind.

I think the Northeast, in general, is more academically focused. Especially in Massachusetts, the university system is such a big industry. Whereas south Florida is influenced heavily by the Hispanic culture, which is more entrepreneurial, less reliant on degrees but more of what you've done.

I was the first one in my family to go to college. Not many of my friends left Florida. If they did go to college, they didn't leave the area, they stayed.

Hanna: So when you left the school you created in Florida, were they mad at you for leaving? Did people feel betrayed?

Dionne: I think the staff were happy to be rid of me. It's really hard, as you know, to run a Sudbury school and to hold the philosophy that kids are capable of educating themselves and solving their own problems and handling their own conflicts, etcetera. A lot of adults think it's neglect when you don't try to guide children or be involved in their issues from day to day. You're supposed to be there as a loving, guiding, caring adult, and I wasn't that. I think I had more respect for the kids and more confidence in their skills. So we had our conflicts around that. I think that's typical; it wasn't unique to us, I'm sure it's a common problem between staff at different Sudbury schools. I was able to hold my ground in the first five years because I knew what vision I had, what I wanted to build, what I wanted for my kids. But once I decided that I was going to move up here, I wasn't willing to fight anymore.

I realized I didn't have any more patience. It wasn't worth fighting anymore. I probably said things a lot more directly. Before I might have said things more politically. I was there part-time because I was pretty much the administration of the school, so I focused on that in my sixth year. I focused on passing everything on to either a parent or a staff member.

Hanna: When you read our literature or came here on visits, and then you came here as a parent and staff, there must have been some things that struck you as not what you expected?

Dionne: The first time I came here, I didn't expect to feel this magical place. You can read about the place and the philosophy and what graduates go on to do, but until you visit you can't feel it. Just being in this place—for me, I can only describe as magical. You encounter kids that are different than most kids you meet out there, that are actually interesting and don't have this fear. They're alive. It's hard to describe for me: everybody here is alive, and yet very respectful, not in your face. I just found the little things like going into the little bathroom in the music study room where two boys were sitting and playing and laughing and immediately they scooted their chairs in so I could easily get through. I'm like, where am I? Just a really respectful place. I felt like I could just be here. Does that make sense? So that was the magic. And then that kept me coming back every year when I was running Sunset in Florida, I knew I needed to come back every year to kind of keep me going, because I did feel lonely down there. It's tough being the one to hold the philosophy, trying to keep it together.

I knew I wanted my children to be here, I was sure about that. I wasn't sure if I wanted to be staff here. This is definitely for my children and I don't want to be in their space. And I know that's going to be hard to maneuver. I'm trying to navigate that;

we don't talk about school that much. I mean they tell me what they've done, I try not to comment, as if I don't know any of these people that they're telling me about. Just so they feel like they have their own space. So when I finally decided I did want to be staff, it was exactly what I expected because I had been here half a dozen times before.

Hanna: Anything that's different now that you are on the staff?

Dionne: Maybe I expected this: I'm definitely less needed here than I was at the small school in Florida. When you only have fifteen kids, the adults that are there are a big part of the community. That was an adjustment for me. Okay, they don't need me, they have each other. So what am I going to do here to still contribute to the school? It took me some time to find my groove. I was surprised at how much time and space the staff has given me to just feel comfortable in the environment and get to know the culture. It took me a while to be able to just sit back and enjoy that—to allow myself to just absorb the culture and not having to do, do, do. I always wonder if this is what a new student feels like at Sudbury Valley. Nobody's telling you what to do, you kind of have to find your way. It's been a struggle. There were times when I'm like, what am I doing here? Why did they invite me to become staff?

Hanna: We're looking for people for the future, and who have organizational competence. We are an educational institution, we also have to run a business that pays the rent, pays the insurance, get the lawn mowed, all the mundane things that every household and every business does, so that's totally not spiritual like helping children be free. But it is spiritual because without doing it, the school won't be here. I think the fact that you ran a school gives you the insight and also makes it hard.

Dionne: It's true. Because I ran a school, I know how hard it is. Not the physical running of it, that's actually the easy part, but the holding this philosophy in place. So I totally admire the people who are here and have been here for fifty years.

I get the feeling that SVS is really stable. I get that feeling from talking to the kids and talking to some of the parents at the Open Houses, or the ones that I see when they come to pick up their kids.

There's a subtle confidence in the school, in the model. In general, you don't have the really nervous parents or the really nervous kid that results from parents not really being supportive of the school—not necessarily every parent and every child—but in general. The families that moved up here along with me from Florida, one thing they always say is when they come to an Open House, they feel like this school is so solid, like it's such a professional institution that's going to be here forever. And that gives them confidence in the school.

Hanna: You could work at high tech, or whatever, as MIT graduates do, and make a lot more money. So why are you here?

Dionne: You're right, I can work anywhere else. I feel like I can. And projects come and go and sometimes they're challenging so it's fun for a while. I can get immersed in a project. But, at the end of the day, what am I really doing? It's not fulfilling for my soul. I know that sounds totally cheesy.

Hanna: It's amazing that the most important thing in your life, beside your family, is being lucky enough to get an occupation that fits your soul. And to say so is considered almost indecent in our society because most people are not lucky enough to have that.

Dionne: Yeah. It's fulfilling. Of course. Even with all the heartache and headache at Sunset and the drama, there was not one day I woke up and said I don't feel like going to school today. That's really powerful. For the first five years I never said that. I had been in so many different jobs before that, and at least once a month I'd call in sick. I'd just call in: I'm not going to work that day. And I've been here since September and it hasn't happened here.

Hanna: Do you find it interesting here?

Dionne: Yes. What is interesting? Wow, where do I start? I think all the students are interesting, definitely. I've always been interested in how—and now I'm totally going to sound cheesy—you, Danny and Mimsy have continued for fifty years—that's amazing to me, it really is. There's some secret sauce there that I need to learn.

Hanna: I don't know. I used to say that as soon as my kids graduate, I'm outta here. And my youngest child is 46. So, obviously, I've been staying here long beyond that. Danny, Mimsy and Mikel all have grown children who have finished at the school, and we all still want to be here. For me, I believe in the philosophy, I think it's important work beyond being just satisfying for me personally. It satisfies me that I'm dedicating my work life to a worthwhile cause.

I think that all kids deserve to be trusted, respected and given the same kind of human rights that we extend to all adults in this country—at least theoretically. And I'm very sad, because it seems to me that that's being a bit eroded in the last period of time with the parents being more helicopter parenting, they have less trust in their children. They think they're being good to their children, I think they're being very bad to their children. I don't think it's loving. I think real love is to trust your kid, not to tell them what to do every five minutes.

Dionne: This is the school that I wanted to go to when I was younger. And I think this is how children should be treated. I made a decision long before I found Sudbury that I wanted to work with kids. That's important to me, that's the future. I want to make an impact, and maybe it's selfish. But I think this is the answer. That reminds me of a saying: build a life that you don't need a vacation from.

Mimsy Sadofsky

"I like solving problems. There's always a new problem to solve. I don't ever feel like my work is the same one year as it was the year before . . . if you're lucky enough to be doing something that is meaningful to you, that allows you to feel that the world can be bettered by it—not by what I do, but by what the school produces—that's a very exciting thing."

Hanna: You've been here since the very beginning of the school. What was it that made you interested in this kind of school?

Mimsy: Well, Mike and I had a child. We actually had two children, but one of them was just a regular child. Our oldest child was quite clear from the moment of birth about his own agenda. There was never any give and take. He knew what he needed, he knew when he needed it, and he was very stubborn when he was asked to deviate. So he was very excited about going to school, but when he went to first grade it was crushing because he discovered that all the things that he wanted to learn were slowly and competitively taught. There was a lot of group responsibility for things like somebody talking out of turn, which he didn't do.

Hanna: Did he go to kindergarten?

Mimsy: He went to kindergarten. It was very exciting because we lived in Rome, New York, and the school bus stop, to which he went on his own every day, was about a quarter mile from our house. He would put on his snow boots—in Rome it's pretty much always snowy—and he would run down the street as fast as he could. He was quite sure that the minute he could take his snow boots off he'd be able to fly, because he practiced so much. He would practice on the swing sets. It turned out in the end that he couldn't fly, but he didn't mind kindergarten. He hated nursery school, and he was a nursery school dropout after just a few days.

Hanna: So he went to public school. Where?

Mimsy: Sudbury. We moved to Sudbury so that he could have really good public schools. That's why we chose Sudbury.

Hanna: Did he know how to read already?

Mimsy: No. Strange but true.

Hanna: So what bothered him?

Mimsy: What bothered him was that the readers were put into groups. They were the bluebirds and the blackbirds and the red birds and the whatever birds. But it was clear which group had the most skilled students in it, so he couldn't stop himself from wanting to be, and getting to be, in the most highly skilled group. And that was very, very painful for him; he ended up getting very close to ulcers.

Hanna: My memory of him is reading all the time.

Mimsy: That's what he did. It's surprising that he didn't learn sooner, but he didn't. And he didn't get ulcers but he was definitely on the way. He had constant stomach aches, and he got a little depressed. We knew this couldn't be right, because we knew that we had produced a perfect little child! So we knew that he was fine, and we said: what's wrong here? We started reading the

John Holt books and there were all kinds of other books that were being put out at that time. It was early in 1968. We said: maybe there's another way. Then at just about the same time—the spring or the winter of 1968—someone told me about this group that was forming a new school in Framingham and maybe I'd want to look into it. It was just a few months before the school opened. I wasn't really a *founder* founder, because I did not join until that spring, but don't tell anybody.

So I came to some sort of public meeting. It took place in the sewing room and there were a lot of people. The school just seemed like a good idea. The less intervention in the child's life that wasn't necessary, the better, as our son had taught us very early on.

Hanna: But you and Mike were both good students.

Mimsy: Well, I was a moderately good student. Mike was a naughty student. But neither one of us was stupid. Once we had read the literature about schooling that was popular at the time, we never had doubts about how to do things with our children.

Hanna: Did you discuss child rearing when you were dating?

Mimsy: When I was dating I was eighteen and nineteen, I didn't even know what children were. I had never babysat. I don't even think Mike knew anything about children.

Hanna: So it's really fortuitous that you happened to come to the same conclusions once you had a child.

Mimsy: No, it wasn't fortuitous. I don't think you're remembering Hal too well. Hal was the guide from the beginning. He taught us how to be parents; he taught us everything.

Hanna: So we opened in the summer. Did you come? Did Hal come in the summer?

Mimsy: We were away in July. We had planned that long before. We came to the summer session around August 1st.

Hanna: Was he happy here?

Mimsy: He was very happy, and so was Debra, our second child. But in September he said, "I don't think I'm going to be able to learn everything I need to know in this school, I want to go back to public school." You can't imagine how furious I was at that child. It was the most embarrassing thing that happened to me in my entire life. So I said, "You take care of that, you're seven now." I took him to the public school, and he re-enrolled. Then after less than a week he said, "I was wrong." And I said, "You were wrong, you take care of that. You go to Dennis Flynn, and you talk to him about it and you figure out what to do next." At the time, Dennis was handling enrollments.

Hanna: But you're still driving this child. He didn't go by himself, you brought him here.

Mimsy: I was working and I was driving his sister.

Hanna: So once he accepted it the second time around, could you verbalize what he thought to himself?

Mimsy: I don't really know. I think he thought that he was very lucky to be in a position to discover things on his own and to be with people who were fun.

Hanna: And the worry about learning everything he needed, did it stay with him?

Mimsy: It did not stay with him at all. It was gone.

Hanna: One of the things that Amy Wilson, who was a friend of theirs, said to me was that the best part of the school for her was that all the kids in her group were so brilliant and interesting and creative.

Mimsy: That's true of groups now; they feel the same way. Do you think Amy knew it at the time? Now we look back and are very sure about it. Because I didn't even know it at the time. In the first years of the school, for a long time, I did not understand that we basically only have brilliant students. I didn't understand it for a very long time.

Hanna: Why do you think that's so?

Mimsy: Because I always feel that their brains are very quick—they're very sharp and they see things. They're just brilliant, all of them. The littlest kids will have conversations with you which make your jaw drop open. And a lot of the big kids do things that big kids don't do in high school, which is really good for all of them. If somebody is reading a really intellectual book and they're in a room with other people, it's not just an accident that some conversation goes on, and some realization of what the intellectual world is.

Hanna: I always wonder whether only parents who have the children like this have the courage to send them here—that we do have some kind of self-selection.

Mimsy: I've wondered that too, and I don't know the answer.
I think that is true to a certain extent. But if you think about the parents of the seven and eight year olds, they're pretty varied. The kids are varied too. But I do think they have parents who actually think about education. That's not necessarily true for older kids. They're really nice kids, but I think a lot of them are here because the parents couldn't figure out where to put them.

Hanna: So you had friends about your age and they had kids. Now that you were jumping out of your social circle, what happened?

Mimsy: Well, two things happened. One is that we lost our friends, slowly but surely. But the other thing that happened was that in November of the first year, 1968, we moved away for almost two years and so during that time we sort of finished losing our friends around here.

Hanna: Where did you go?

Mimsy: First, we went to Washington, DC, for about nine months, and then we went to Houston to NASA for a year. Then we came back here because it was just not working out with the children.

Hanna: So your children went to regular school again. How was that?

Mimsy: Well, I think that's a very interesting thing. I think that even in a few months here, children get a certain feeling about their own identity that they keep with them when they leave. So, when a teacher says to you that you should be doing such and such, it's not as hard as it was before to have it bounce off of you. You've got enough of a feeling of who you are, and that you should be respected. I don't know how it happens so fast, but it does. So it was not as bad as before, but it was still bad for Hal, and it was not even good for Debra, because it's not good to go to other schools. When we first moved to Texas, Debra was about to turn six, and she had been to kindergarten. The kindergarten she went to didn't teach them to read. There was a lady who lived next door to us in Texas, a first grade teacher, and she said about Debra, "She won't be able to go to first grade because she can't read." Looking at this child, who's about six inches taller than everybody else her age, I said: "oh yes she will." Of course she did. And read very quickly. It's not rocket science, reading.

Hanna: So did the kids talk about Sudbury Valley when you were away?

Mimsy: Yes, and they told other kids about it too.

Hanna: So for your kids what this school offered was clearer than for my kids, because my kids never went to regular school. Do you think when you came back, they cherished what this school offered?

Mimsy: They cherish it now. They're very grateful, and very grateful to all of the founders. It's a big deal, and they know it's a big deal.

Hanna: Part of it is that we're also close. It isn't only an institutional thing.

Mimsy: No, it's not at all only an institutional thing, but it's certainly also an institutional thing, and they're very clear on how it's an institutional thing. At one point in her adulthood, Debra was working in some job that was a fine job, and she said: Sudbury Valley people just can't "settle". They have to have what they want, they have to have the things that are important and meaningful to them. Because otherwise, you'd just be a cog in a machine. These are the people who push boundaries, people who think like that and are like that.

Hanna: Was Hal showing any aptitude for math, or interest in math, when he was a little kid?

Mimsy: Of course. It wasn't interest so much. He knew how to do things with numbers. Numbers were not interesting to him because they were so clear. All three of my children are very mathematical. Somebody gave Hal a box of cuisinaire rods when he was six. He opened it up and he wrote the number on every rod and he then put it away. That was it. He was done. They weren't going to teach him anything.

Hanna: What's so fun for me is that Hal and Miki and Talya and Debra and Seth and David were all close friends. And they're entirely different. But they had a lot in common and they could talk forever.

Mimsy: They still can.

Hanna: So I think that even though this school was small, they were very interesting to each other, because each kid had so much of their own character. They always had interesting conversations.

Mimsy: I think that's how people feel now about the kids here.

Hanna: So the fact that they were interested in different things was a plus. They didn't share the interest, but they shared their knowledge, and that was very nice for them.

So now you're staff. You went to college and you majored in literature. What did you do here?

Mimsy: Actually while we were gone, while we lived in Washington, I did a lot of library work for the school. About once a week I would spend a day at the Library of Congress finding information for the books here. It was when we were cataloging our books.

Hanna: So when your children enrolled, you became staff right away. How did you become staff? How did it work?

Mimsy: I think it was because it sounded like fun, and it seemed interesting, and it seemed like there would be things that I could do when the school was getting started that probably I wouldn't be doing afterwards. I thought I might be helpful with administrative work and office work and stuff like that but I never thought I would have anything to do with kids in a sort of teaching role. It never occurred to me to be a teacher, and it never occurred to me that I liked children. I liked my children just fine, but these were not things I was thinking about. So I thought: ok, I'll work there until they don't need me anymore. And I figured it would just be a couple of years.

Hanna: We weren't paying any salaries. So you thought you would help this institution get established?

Mimsy: Yes, but I did not think it in an unprofessional way. I thought of it as real work. I didn't think oh, maybe I'll come on Tuesday and not on Wednesday.

Hanna: So you immediately worked full-time?

Mimsy: I think I did, but I can't remember. But the point is that I did not consider it sort of, "Oh, let's help out at the new school." I considered it an enterprise that was worth getting off the ground and doing anything I could to make it go.

Hanna: And the fact that you weren't earning any money, was that a problem at all for you or Mike?

Mimsy: No. We never fight about money. We've never had a fight about money or children in our lives. Don't worry, we can still fight, plenty.

Hanna: A marriage works when you agree about the big things and the fights are usually about little things.

Mimsy: Yes. So I thought it was very exciting.

I had been nagging to leave the area for a long time. I'd been saying I didn't want to live in the Boston area anymore. When we first moved to Boston, Mike was in graduate school at Northeastern and we had a very different idea of what life was going to be like than what it turned out to be. The apartments that we lived in were almost disgusting. I found the whole Massachusetts scene to be dark and foreboding, so I was constantly talking about moving. And it just happened that the moving happened just as I became happy with a job here and then I couldn't go back because Mike changed companies. It took a couple of years to work back in.

Hanna: So basically you were here in the beginning and then you took about two years off and then you came back at the beginning of the third year. What was the feeling when you came back here?

Mimsy: I don't remember it terribly well. It seemed like where the children and I should be—that I understood. But I don't know what the feeling was. There were some discomforts in it for me. I can't tell what, but I wasn't that comfortable a lot of the time here. I was always worried that I was not that useful for quite a few years, but then if you work hard enough, you become useful because people think what you do is important, because you do it.

But people were nice. I liked the kids a lot here. The staff were a little quirky at that point. They didn't bother me, they were just plain quirky.

Hanna: The first years anybody who wanted to be staff could be staff. We didn't put any hurdles. You say you want to be staff, you can be staff.

Mimsy: When I came back, that wasn't true. I was elected. I wrote to the school and said I was coming back and my name was put into the election pool.

Hanna: Ever since we started the school to this very day, we get attached to certain kids and then the parents pull them out for all kinds of reasons—financial, philosophical mainly. Was that very stressful for you?

Mimsy: For me, yes. I find it very stressful now, because I'm always wanting enrollment to be bigger and wanting these people to understand what the school is and why it's good the way it is. So, it's very stressful to this very day. I've always fought verbally to help parents understand why they shouldn't do that. I usually lose, but very occasionally, we win.

Hanna: Why do you think this school is so terrific for kids?

Mimsy: Because I think that kids are human beings—*people*. And the school treats them like people and not like little cute things. It allows them to grow up and develop and flower into who they are. That's why I think it's so terrific. I think that when young children come here, or even middle-aged children, you see that very clearly. When older children come, I think they catch it from the younger children to some extent—not always, but to some extent. The younger children are models for them and they catch that sort of wholeness of person and respect for themselves, and respect for everybody else. It's hard for me to believe that I walk in here and kids treat me like I'm twenty-five, in some ways. They'll talk to me about things—their games, the books they read—they're just regular people. And I'm a regular person and I don't think I'd be a regular person if I wasn't here. I'd be an old person maybe.

Hanna: At Sudbury Valley, we value the individual and we tell them to develop their own selves. Society-at-large has a body of knowledge that it wants to impart to children to preserve the culture and to prepare them for successful adulthood. Why do you think that's not important?

Mimsy: I think that the body of knowledge that each person needs for a successful adulthood is individual. There is no way for every person to get all of the body of knowledge that people think they should have. Instead, they aim like homing pigeons towards the parts of it that they need or want. Now why is that good? You've interviewed a lot of alumni. Don't they tell you that it's good?

Hanna: Yes. These are the kids that we keep. I know that we lose a lot of kids.

Mimsy: And sometimes parents don't give their children a chance because they're too worried about whether they'll be able to get into the right college or the wrong college or any college. Or they're too worried about whether they'll pass the MCAS, which we don't have here, and how well they'll do on the SATs . . .

Hanna: It's development of the self *vs.* the accumulation of knowledge.

Mimsy: But I think you accumulate so much knowledge here. For instance, who knew that Seth would know how to spell. Seth just read. He read all the time. He didn't write. Who knew he would know how to spell? You don't know how to spell so well.

Hanna: I don't think it has anything to do with reading.

Mimsy: I don't either. So it occurred to me that it was sort of strange that he knew how to spell. When I asked him, he said, "It was because I was the Scrabble champion at school." Now,

I never knew he was the Scrabble champion at school! He's also very competitive, which all my children are, but they don't admit it.

Hanna: Actually, I'm a bad speller and a great reader and I think it has something to do with how you look at words when you are reading. And I guess I don't see the gestalt of the word.

Mimsy: I shouldn't have said "spelling". He understands parts of speech and how sentences are made. And it turns out that all the kids who go to school here do, to some extent.

Hanna: Is he a good writer?

Mimsy: I have no idea. Seth can write anything he wants to say in one or two sentences. I don't know if he ever writes a lot. But he's certainly very good at expressing himself verbally—very, very good, and very careful with his words. He doesn't ever waste any. But he does understand how sentences are put together and what adverbs are and all those weird things.

Hanna: So you have three different kids and all of them know different things, right?

Mimsy: No, they all know the same things. They all read the same books. Their personalities are more diverse.

Hanna: So how do you think the kids here get self-esteem? Because if your kids went to public school, they would be very good students hopefully and they would measure against all typical American kids, or their neighbor, or they would get self-esteem that way—maybe, or maybe not. How do the kids here get self-esteem?

Mimsy: By trying and failing and trying again. By learning that they can do things on their own.

Hanna: And you think the students here are aware of it?

Mimsy: I think sometimes they are. I think sometimes by the time they graduate they are aware of it. But in general, I don't know. I was talking to seven-year-old Charlie, who went skiing with his dad in Colorado for a few days last week. I said to him beforehand, "Are you a good skier?" He answered, "Of course!" And what he meant was that he's skied a lot, and he knows darn well that he's a good skier. But it wasn't like he was bragging; it was like: "That's the way it is. I am. I've had that experience, I know it, I'm on top of it." And I think that's the way people here are with a lot of things.

Hanna: You don't think they worry that kids in the neighborhood know stuff that they don't?

Mimsy: Sometimes. My kids didn't. I think my kids knew stuff that the other kids in the neighborhood didn't know. And I think most of the kids in this school do. So if the kids in the neighborhood know all the capitols of the States, for instance, big deal. But the kids who go to school here know all kinds of things. Graham, who is six years old, knows how to sentence people and how to get truthful testimony out of people in JC!

Hanna: So now it's 50 years that you're working at the school, and we all seem to work hard, and are very dedicated. And you especially work hard and are dedicated. What is it that keeps you going?

Mimsy: I guess I like what I'm doing.

Hanna: You do a lot of different things, so what are you talking about?

Mimsy: Well, my favorite thing to do is to talk to parents. My very favorite thing to do is to interview, and my second favorite thing to do is to interact with parents, which there's a lot of, besides the interviewing. And I very much like the amount of writing that I do, which is not an enormous amount, but it's a useful amount. And I like editing, and putting together publications, which are probably totally useless because the world doesn't read anymore—it's an interactive world. And I like solving problems. There's always a new problem to solve. I don't ever feel like my work is the same one year as it was the year before. I can't tell you why. Like right now, as you definitely know, all year we have been working to solve and to be careful about and to worry about fiscal problems. We have worked to be even more cautious than usual about spending. There are always plenty of problems—how to get a book published inexpensively, how to word an invitation—silly things, little things and big things. I like them all. I like working on the web page because I'm very excited about it and proud of it and I think it's going to represent us very well in the world. I felt the old one was terrible. I've been saying for years that all I want for the fiftieth anniversary is a new web page. And we had to hold back on it last year because of money. It's very expensive. People say: why are you doing that? You can just do a nice little web page yourselves. But I really think it's a very beautiful thing.

Hanna: Then why do we do it?

Mimsy: Because you can't do a nice web page yourself. You can just do a boring little web page yourself. That's why.

Hanna: And you think that's how you get new students, from the web page?

Mimsy: I don't know. I have no idea how we get new students. I think it's word of mouth, but I think it's word of mouth and word of the internet, both. I mean, you hear about something and you go look it up. You want to see what it is. You find out all sorts of things about it that you wouldn't necessarily have bothered to find twenty years ago or more, when you would have had to go to the library. Now it's right in front of you. All the time. It's even on your phone.

Hanna: Do you feel that in order to have a satisfying life, you have to have a meaning to it that's more than just survival—more than having a relationship, having kids, feeding them, taking care of them?

Mimsy: It's hard to say this because there's an awful lot of people in the world who have to struggle just to survive. But if you're lucky enough to be doing something that is meaningful to you, that allows you to feel that the world can be bettered by it—not by what I do, but by what the school produces—that's a very exciting thing.

Hanna: I know that you've also been very active with helping start-up groups all over the world. Do you find that satisfying?

Mimsy: Yes. Extremely. But it's also sort of sad, because most people run into big problems. Also people that you work very hard with often turn out not to like you.

Hanna: Why do you think that?

Mimsy: I don't know why, and it's a shock to me that people find me or the school annoying or off-putting. Maybe it's because this really touches on values. The values here are core values. People don't necessarily like to be told that what they think of as important may not be. People can get very upset when they don't agree with you because they know that it's something coming right out of your heart and your head. So it's like: I can't be with you if I can't talk to you about this and have you agree with me. I think that's how they feel and so they get angry and they walk away. I also think there's a certain amount of jealousy when you get into a larger arena, in the whole group of Sudbury schools.

Hanna: I find working here is a combination of elation and sadness, even heartbreak . . .

Mimsy: Yes, that's very well put. Almost every day there's elation because of the joy in this place, the happiness, the way people behave towards each other, and the way they are always doing something novel. And the heartbreak is sort of endless because more people do not come, and those who come don't necessarily stay, or they don't necessarily have parents who allow them to really develop. That's the kind of heartbreak I feel. Sometimes I just feel that we've been working for so many years and it's still so hard, just plain hard. Don't you ever feel that?

Hanna: Yes. The school seems so "obvious", and it is to some parents and some kids. They walk into the school, they go from the parking lot through the big yard, up the stairs, through some rooms, to the office, and everywhere there are children of all ages. And they all look calm, comfortable with each other. There's a lot of smiling and joking. They're always very polite. They're exuberant without being too loud. And you know how in public school the minute you are out at recess there's a hysterical sound. We don't have that.

Mimsy: Recess, or the end of the day at public school, is like an explosion.

Hanna: We don't have that here, but we have all these kids all over the place. And every parent who comes here went to traditional schools, and they know what that experience is like. Do they not see the kids here? Do they not see that these kids are special?

Mimsy: I think they often think the kids are special. A woman from California that I had interviewed was here this morning with her darling eight year old boy, and she had told Jean on the phone that she wanted to see Sudbury Valley and maybe she wanted to see another school too. But after she was about to leave she said, "I know this is what I want for my son. I realize that I'm just going to have to figure out how to pay for it because this is what I want, and he is going to come here." That was what it was—it was those other kids she saw. I had explained it to her, but that's just words. She saw it.

Hanna: We have visiting students, do you think they see it?

Mimsy: In general, yes. Some visiting students find it too much to handle.

Hanna: So do you feel that you've done something worthwhile with your time when you go home?

Mimsy: Yes, until you think real hard about it. Sometimes it's elation and sometimes it's despair. Yes, generally, but it also depends on how you are feeling about yourself at the moment. I think we're not nearly as evolved as the students in the school. Not nearly as evolved.

Hanna: Do you think that this school is going to be viable in the next fifty years?

Mimsy: I think it's possible. I don't think it will be exactly the same. And I think it will be hard to maintain. To us, it's always a start-up and we're always feeling like this is something new, we have to figure it out. But I don't know if it'll be like that to the next generation. If they can maintain this, or some other even better atmosphere, yes.

Hanna: Do you think this model is a good model for the 21st century in America?

Mimsy: I do. I've thought for a long time that the whole standard educational system would eventually cave in on itself, because it's sort of built on sand; and that people would realize that there were these huge, vast expenditures and that it was not working out.

Hanna: Mimsy, you know for a fact that almost all of our kids who go to college excel. Why do you think that is?

Mimsy: Because they know who they are. Because they are strong. They don't let other people push them around, intellectually.

Hanna: What they tell me is that they're doing it because they want to do it and once they want to do something, they totally focus. That's why they do it so well, whether they have an aptitude for it or not. Do you agree with that?

Mimsy: I do agree with that, but I think that it's not quite that simple. Because the road to what I want is littered with obstacles that I'm not interested in, and I have to get over those obstacles. And that's the same with every kid, in every way.

Hanna: If you want to buy a harpsichord or a guitar and then you have to work at McDonald's to get the money, you do it. It's boring, it's difficult, but you want to do it. We adults also have that. We want to do something, then we find ways to get the resources, and not all those ways are pleasant.

Mimsy: I think most people make an artificial line between the things they do to earn a living and the things they do to make themselves happy. So it may be that knitting is what really is exciting to me and yet I have to earn X thousand dollars a year, so I go and do computer programming. The truth is that I have to do that computer programming so I can knit. It's true on a smaller scale too. So when our graduates do really well in college courses, they're going to have some courses they don't like, and they'll do well, because this is what they have to do.

Hanna: You have used a tremendous amount of your time to help start-up groups all over the world. Why do you think it's for us that you are using the time to do it?

Mimsy: I think in the beginning, when other groups first started to form, and we were working with them, it was good for us to feel like we weren't alone in the world. Also, we met very interesting people, with fascinating ideas. Now, I think it's primarily to help other people to give kids something good in their school lives— even in schools that don't necessarily last. Sacramento Valley School, which was open for more than 20 years and has been closed for quite a while, has a tremendous number of amazing graduates. The more people like this there are, the better. One by one is not so fast, but we're making slow progress in changing the face of education.

Hanna: There was a school like this in Copenhagen, Denmark, and some of those kids were visiting us this year, and they were incredible. So every child, here and there, adds up to lots of people.

Mimsy: They are people who have good lives, or who have a better chance than most people at having a good life, and under-standing their lives and their world.

Hanna: But when you started working here, you weren't trying to change the world. You just were trying to do a good job with the kids that are here.

Mimsy: I was mostly interested in my own personal children, but very quickly I felt that it was an important world endeavor.

Hanna: So are you disappointed?

Mimsy: I don't know if "disappointed" is the right word. I'm sorry that it hasn't happened more. And I'm wondering what's going to happen. I don't think this school is necessarily the kind we're going to have in forty years, and I don't know whether there are going to be schools at all. But I'm not disappointed.

Hanna: What I think about when I come here every day is how lucky I am that I walk into this building and Hayden and Kevin and Ethan and all the little kids say hello, or give me a hug, or give me a cookie, or say "I'm not happy today", or whatever. When I was their age, adults didn't exist, they weren't human beings. Danny always says when the kid says "hi, Danny," it makes his day. So I feel very lucky to be surrounded by real happy, enthusiastic, live people. I really feel good about it.

Mimsy: This morning I was walking down after I left the people who came for an interview, and I was walking back to the building and Michael Doherty was playing basketball and he said, "Hey Mimsy, this basket's for you." What more can you ask for in life?

Hanna: Nothing. Because that kid is twelve years old and he's just been here a short time. He is grateful to you and he knows that because what you're doing somehow gives him freedom. I don't know if he could articulate it, but he did when he said what he said to you. He thanked you for having the school. That was the most beautiful thing. That can make your week, it's more than just a day.

Mimsy: That's right. It did.

Mikel Matisoo

"I can't imagine a way that I could contribute to making a better world than making sure that this institution thrives. There is a quantum difference between people who have been allowed to take responsibility for themselves and have been respected all their lives, and people who have not. We have people who grow up feeling that they are building the world that they are living in, as opposed to accommodating themselves to one that somebody else is running for them."

Hanna: Mikel, do you mind telling me about your own high school and college and how you got here, how you heard about SVS.

Mikel: I went to a lot of different schools when I was growing up—ordinary public schools, private schools, Department of Defense schools. The high school that I went to was a Department of Defense school in Yokosuka, Japan.

Then I came back to the United States to go to college at MIT, when I was eighteen. And the way that I ended up finding out about Sudbury Valley is complicated. I had taken a history class. The class was on the Spanish Civil War and part of what happened there was that anarchist trade unions had arranged what I guess would pass for a government. They had set those up in parts of Spain, and I had gotten interested in them. My history professor was listed in the catalog as teaching a class on the history of anarchism. I was interested in taking the class, but he said he didn't teach it anymore because nobody ever signed up for it. So I told him that I could deliver a bunch of people to register for the class if he would teach it.

I was a junior and knew a lot of people. So he ended up doing the class and a number of the other people in the class were friends of mine. When we got to the point of talking about anarchist educational philosophy, the professor mentioned that there was a school in Framingham that in many ways had an educational philosophy that was consistent with that. I said, "That makes sense; what a good thing!" As it turns out one of my friends who was in the class, David Gould, was much more intrigued by that than I and ended up visiting the school and became a staff member.

When we all left college, in about 1983, we shared a house in Brighton. He was a staff member at Sudbury Valley while we all lived together in that house. I had the opportunity to visit the school a couple of times. I said, "This is great, this is exactly what schools should be." And I didn't give much other thought to it.

Hanna: Were you dissatisfied with your own school experience?

Mikel: I had a very difficult time in school as a small child. Kindergarten wasn't so bad, but by the time I got to first grade I had started having problems. I did not want to do what they wanted me to do, and they didn't seem to be paying a whole lot of attention to what was going on with me. For example, they assumed that I didn't read . The thing was that when I got the reading book, I read everything in it right away.

Finally someone asked me why I wasn't interested in reading. I said, "I read the book when you first gave it to me and it wasn't interesting anymore." So at least in that case, they gave me different reading books. But I still had a lot of trouble. They wanted me to sit at a desk and I wanted to walk around and talk to people and look out the window.

Hanna: So you came to school and were you bored or you just didn't like to sit?

Mikel: Well, at first I would get bored, and then I would come up with some way to amuse myself. That usually got me in trouble. So my parents tried a private school. This was very early in the awareness of what they originally called "minimal cerebral dysfunction", and then that became "hyperactivity". It's what we now know as ADHD. They decided that was an issue for me, and they put me on dexadrine and I took dexadrine daily until I was ten.

Hanna: What did you think of that at the time as a kid?

Mikel: I got in trouble less—that was my awareness of it. I was in trouble all the time before I started taking it, and I was only in trouble some of the time once I was on it. And the teachers seemed to notice some sort of a difference because they would often ask me if I had forgotten to take it.

Hanna: What do you think it did?

Mikel: I'm not really sure. Maybe it allowed me to find interest in boring, repetitive tasks for a little bit longer. But I always had a difficult time with that. In math, for example, they would show us how to add columns of numbers, and I would understand what they said and I would do it. Then I very quickly got bored of it, but day after day they would give us pages of problems to do and I could not bring myself to do them. Then, of course, because I hadn't finished my math problems, I wouldn't be allowed to go outside for recess, I'd have to sit in the classroom and do math problems. I really didn't like that very much.

As time went on I had learned how to deal with the authoritarian and coercive structures of traditional education. But I had trouble. Through junior high school I still didn't do what people told me to do, but I understood that disrupting the class was going to get me in trouble. So I just didn't do my homework. Some teachers gave me a lot of trouble about that, and others kind of let me go. Then I started getting teachers who let me do what I wanted to do. They let me read books that I wanted to read. A math teacher let me separate from what the class was doing and do my own self-paced math, and that worked fairly well for me. A lot of the teachers I had were interesting, sincere, well-meaning, open-minded people, and quite a few of them made an effort to help me accommodate to what was going on. By the time I got in high school—I went to a very small school— there was a lot of freedom, a lot of flexibility, and I had a lot of free time that I spent in the library.

Hanna: So Mikel, jumping back now to college, do you think that those memories were important reasons for you to become interested in the anarchist course?

Mikel: A lot of what various anarchist theorists talked about in terms of education is not that there's no order, but that there is already an order, and that it doesn't need to be externally imposed, that the rest of nature is able to get along without a lot of externally imposed coercion. It seemed strange to them that we felt that human children could not develop without having somebody telling them what to do and even taking it so far as to separate them from the rest of everyday life and put them in a place where experts had decided what they were going to do all day in order to learn the things they needed to learn to grow up. The idea was that if you let people alone and let them interact with society as they saw fit, that they would educate themselves as they needed to in order to take their place in society.

Hanna: I'm going to ask you a different question, but it's related. Your father was an officer in the Navy, and the military is very hierarchical, right? So you hung out with officers' children mostly?

Mikel: No, with all different kids.

Hanna: Was there social pressure to go to "a good college"?

Mikel: Yes. My mother was from a family where women went to college in the late 19th century.

My parents always told me that I was going to go to college. It wasn't *if* you go to college, it was *when* you go to college. So I always just assumed that I would go to college.

Hanna: So you had good grades.

Mikel: Part of me wanted to get good grades. I used to do nerdy things like argue about things that had been marked wrong on a test where I thought they were right. Things that I cared about, I wanted to do well, and things I didn't really care about, I didn't care as much. Part of what gave me the freedom that I was enjoying was the fact that I was generally doing well in school. For example, I used to make a deal with math teachers, in particular, where I wouldn't have to come to class and I wouldn't have to do homework; that they would grade me just on the test scores. That allowed me, for example, to have an early morning band class that was scheduled at the same time as the Algebra 2 class, so I wouldn't have to worry about showing up for that one. By the time I was eleven or twelve, I had come to an accommodation, I think, with most of the teachers that I had.

From my point of view, I've always been very curious in what I guess most people would regard as an academic direction. I liked history, I liked science, I enjoyed reading literature, those kinds of things I always pursued on my own, just out of curiosity. And I enjoyed math in the sense of learning how to solve puzzles, so that learning how to do mathematical things was like puzzle-solving to me. As long as it was something that was a new puzzle, I was intrigued by it, and I applied myself to it. The issue that I generally had was going back and doing things that I already knew how to do.

Hanna: When did you get married?

Mikel: 1985. A couple of years after college.

Hanna: Your wife is from New York City. So you moved to New York City?

Mikel: No, I shared a house with a bunch of people the year following college and I looked around for work to do. I had passed the exam to be an emergency medical technician and was offered a job as an EMT, but they said you'll have to cut off your beard and your hair. At that point in my life, somehow that seemed like a huge encroachment on my personal freedom, and I chose not to go that route. Looking back at it, it seems kind of silly, but that was the way I felt about it at the time, so I started doing odd jobs. I had always enjoyed trees and flowers and landscaping and those kinds of things. In fact, I cross-registered to take a horticulture class at Wellesley College because they didn't have things like that at MIT. There are also lots of girls there. Actually, interestingly enough, I had also cross-registered for a child development class there. I was already thinking about kids and education. And as part of that class I ended up with a volunteer job at the Wellesley Child Study Center.

Hanna: You were a biology major. MIT had a very nice biology research. Why didn't you decide to be a biologist or get a Ph.D. and do research?

Mikel: That was my plan at a certain point. I did very well in the required biology lab. I think typically you took it as a junior. They offered me a job as a teaching assistant in that lab the following year. I worked for a woman who had a Ph.D. from Yale in molecular biology, but she had gotten married and had a kid and stepped off the academic escalator at that point. Despite the fact that she was obviously very competent, the job that she was able to get when she got back to academia, after getting divorced, was basically doing the same thing that I was doing. She supervised me, but we basically did the same job, which was running this undergraduate biology lab.

That was when I saw the pyramidal nature of academia. I realized that if you wanted to continue to advance, you needed to continue to produce, and there was a lot of pressure to do that. At the same time, I developed more and more a sense of academia as really an ivory tower that was separate from the rest of human life. I decided that what I did not want to experience was more of the same. I didn't really have that much of a problem with competition in academia. I thought that I probably could do the Ph.D. work, but I also realized that I would have to put aside a lot of other things. And I realized that the thing that I wanted really to experience in my life was being married and having a family—that that was the thing that I really wanted to make sure that I got an opportunity to do.

The thing that drew me to biology is that it was the study of life: what is the essence of this whole thing? I got a degree in biology but I took a lot of classes in history and psychology also, trying to pursue this thing about what is human life about. Looking at the big picture of human life, I realized that the thing that most people experience about it is having a family, being in a family, being married and having children and doing that kind of thing.

Hanna: So you left the academic world because you wanted to be part of the mainstream of life. And then you met your wife.

Mikel: Right. She was one of the people living in that house. We moved to California after a while. Our first child, Daniel, was born in California. I had been working for a company in Boston that did interior landscaping. I would go from office to office, basically, taking care of the plants. It was actually a very interesting job in the sense that you got to see a lot of different places as a fly on the wall. I worked in the John Hancock tower up on the very top floors, taking care of the chairman and CEO's offices. I worked at Mass General Hospital, Mass Eye and Ear Infirmary, Logan Airport, a bunch of restaurants, hotels, stock brokerage firms, a lot of different places. I got to see a lot of different people at work. It was a fascinating job in that sense. The caring for the plants part was fairly simple most of the time.

Hanna: Did people talk to you?

Mikel: Yes. Different people talked to me differently. I recall one person in one of those corner offices in some big financial institution who actually said to me, "Why am I doing this instead of doing what you're doing?" I told him that probably what I was doing wouldn't pay his bills and he agreed that that was probably true.

Hanna: Was the pay good?

Mikel: No. It was okay; you could live on it at the time. By then my wife-to-be and I shared an apartment in Boston. The money that we were making doing our respective jobs was enough to pay the rent and buy groceries. It was $5 an hour, which wasn't very much. So I had been doing that and I was aware of the fact that while I was making $5 an hour, they were billing my time at $40 an hour, and I thought that I should be able to make a go of having a business like this. So we headed out to California. My intention was that I would try and start a business.

Hanna: Your parents lived in California.

Mikel: Yes. As it turned out, I needed to start working fairly soon after getting back there. Obviously starting a business is not the kind of thing that brings you a living income at the beginning. So I ended up getting a job in a commercial greenhouse, growing indoor tropical plants. I figured I would use that as a stepping stone to build a business. But staying home, especially with an infant, my wife became very homesick for her family. She had a very close family. Being on the other side of the country was very hard for her, and I think it was very hard for her family as well. This was the first grandchild in the family. There was also another factor that made moving more of a possibility. They told us that they were hiring teachers in New York City without any education background—that all you need is a college degree, especially if you are in math or science, and you can get a temporary teaching certificate and start to work. And they were paying the vast sum of about $22,000 a year, which was a fair amount of money, and it included really good union-type benefits— medical and dental and all of that kind of stuff. So we went back across the country to Brooklyn and I worked for a little while doing landscaping for the rich and famous in Manhattan for a company there, while I took care of the things I needed to do to start working as a public school teacher. I guess we got back there in April. And in September I had a job teaching high school biology at a public school in Williamsburg in Brooklyn. I did that for a couple of years.

Hanna: What kind of neighborhood was that?

Mikel: It was a typical lower income urban neighborhood.

Hanna: Were they interested in your class?

Mikel: It was a fairly dysfunctional school, in that most of the kids who attended did not graduate, and many of the kids in my class had already failed biology a couple of years previously and were taking it for the second or third time. They were not very interested in my class. The kids were good-natured, and they had no real animosity towards me. If I made the class entertaining enough, they would participate.

The dogma in the Board of Education at that time was something called "the developmental lesson", where you would write a question on the board at the beginning of the class, and then you would ask the class questions to elicit the components of an outline that would bring the class to an end by answering the question that you had put on the board. The idea is that you build on the previous syllabus, and so it relied a lot on kids paying attention and learning that stuff. They weren't so good at that part, so I kind of modified it in the direction of being more like charades: I would be looking for a particular word.

Hanna: So Mikel did it have meaning for you to do that work? Or did you suffer?

Mikel: I did not feel like I suffered particularly. It was a job that allowed me to support my family. At that point, and I guess for most of my life, I have found that a meaningful thing. And I really did enjoy the subject matter. It was always something that I had found intriguing and beautiful. The problem of trying to communicate it to people who were not as interested in it as I was was an interesting problem. Every day I had to come up with a lesson plan and figure out how I was going to cover this particular piece of the syllabus and that was kind of interesting. I got to know the material myself much better.

Hanna: How long did you stay in that school?

Mikel: Two years. The second year they didn't have enough biology classes for me to have a schedule that was all biology, but they wanted me to stay on as a teacher. So they asked me if I could also teach general science and fundamental math. I ended up doing that.

I think two years was the right amount of time. I don't think I would have been happy doing that for a lot longer. The kids were interesting. There were probably five percent of the kids who were immigrants from Poland, or various African countries, or the Dominican Republic, and those kids actually tended to be much more interested in doing well in school. Then there were some very intelligent kids who were not interested in doing well in school that were also happy to explain to me the world as they saw it, and what they saw as their pathway to whatever their success was going to be. A lot of them offered very interesting critiques of what was wrong and why it wasn't working. In general, the assistant principals I worked for were good people, who were trying to do the very best they could with the resources that they had and were very easy people to work for. I was brand new at all of this and they were very supportive.

Hanna: Then what happened?

Mikel: Well, at the end of my second year, our second child was born. So we had an infant and a two-year-old, and we needed to start thinking about where they were going to grow up and how they were going to grow up.

It was clear to me that I was not going to spend my future as a public school teacher; that it was an interesting interlude, but that it was really quite a dysfunctional system. There wasn't really any future there for me, plus I never really believed in it either.

Hanna: You're saying that not because it was an underprivileged part of society?

Mikel: The fact that it was so dysfunctional had to do with the fact that it was a less privileged segment of society. I think that if I had been in some highly regarded suburban school system, I would have liked it less, because there would have been a lot more pressure. That was one aspect of it being an underperforming school, it was hard to screw things up. So sincere effort was all that people were looking for, and I think that made it easier. It also made it much clearer to me that I really didn't believe in that particular model of education. I did not think it was efficient.

I would have said at the very beginning that I didn't really believe in it. But as far as a job that I could do that would support my family and allow us to move back to New York and make my life happy, it worked very well. But it wasn't something I felt like I could really dedicate myself to. Not only that but we had decided that New York City is a very interesting place to live, but it didn't seem like a very good place to raise kids. At that time, the friend of mine who was on the staff at Sudbury Valley had told me that he was planning on moving on. We talked about it and decided that maybe we would like to try to move up to Massachusetts and get a job at Sudbury Valley and that our kids would go to school there.

Hanna: Antoinette obviously agreed with that. You were in agreement about child rearing.

Mikel: Yes. She did not have an enjoyable time in school.

Hanna: When you were dating, did you discuss child rearing?

Mikel: Yes. For me, it goes without saying that if you're going to marry somebody and have kids with them, that it's a good idea to be pretty much in agreement about the real fundamentals.

I have always had a very difficult time doing things that really went against my grain. If I feel like something is the right thing to do, I'm willing to put a lot of energy into it. And if it's not the right thing to do, I have a very, very difficult time doing it.

Hanna: But it meant that she was going to leave her family again.

Mikel: She didn't mind having a little bit of distance from her family. In a lot of ways I think our marriage has been sort of a hybrid of her very close family and my very less close waspy kind of family.

Fortunately the spring vacation at Sudbury Valley was a different week than the spring vacation at the school where I was working in New York. So I was able to come up and visit for a week. It was very serendipitous because Sudbury Valley had just had a significant spike in enrollment right about that time.

Hanna: Can you recall your first impressions on seeing the building and the grounds and the school ambiance?

Mikel: It was a rainy day in March. The grounds were beautiful, the building was beautiful. Perhaps they had a certain genteel shabbiness to them, but they certainly fit their purpose. Talking to the kids was really like coming home. I think it was because they seemed to enjoy being where they were. They were ingenuous youth, they were just kids being kids. They had conversations with you immediately and talked to you like you were a human being.

Hanna: The pay wasn't the same as the pay in New York, was it?

Mikel: The pay wasn't that different. But there were no benefits. That makes a big difference. I actually had a three-day contract which wasn't really enough to live on. As it turned out, my wife had a friend from college whose family had a lumberyard in Worcester and they had a mill in the lumberyard where they custom millwork. They had a very skilled carpenter working in the mill. One of the things that needs to be done in a lumber mill is cleaning up sawdust, and they had been getting in a certain amount of trouble from their insurance company about the amount of sawdust that had accumulated in their mill. So they were looking for someone just to keep that clean so that the skilled carpenter didn't have to do it. While I was there, he showed me how to operate all of the woodworking machines, so for me it was fascinating because there were lots of new things to learn. By the middle of that school year, I was offered another two days at SVS.

Hanna: Did you feel comfortable right away?

Mikel: Yes, I think I did. I was very young at the time. It was really the kids who taught me how to be a staff member at Sudbury Valley. When I started doing things like going on camping trips, they explained how the stoves worked and the lanterns and they showed me everything. They showed me about JC. It was really the older kids at the school who taught me. They told me how we do things here.

Hanna: How many years have you been here now?

Mikel: It'll be thirty in September.

Hanna: Now you are not learning new things from kids. What keeps you at it?

Mikel: I think I'm still learning new things from kids. I said earlier that I was interested in biology because I really wanted to learn about life, and that is always an opportunity here. That in addition to learning how to be a better staff member all the time, which I feel like I'm still learning. The school is a microcosm and pretty much there are so many things about life that the school connects to.

Hanna: You're going to have to be more articulate.

Mikel: This is a school for people learning about the real world. It's full of all different kinds of people, and of people in interaction with each other, so there is social activity going on all the time. As a staff member you very often get a ringside seat for all of these kinds of human interactions that are going on: there's all the kids, and the kids have parents, and there's this interplay all the time of all of these different people.

The school is on a beautiful piece of land that has trees and grass and a pond and all of those kinds of things so you get to observe nature all the time.

There's a building that needs to have things fixed and grounds that need to have things fixed and that sort of thing goes on all the time.

It's a business that has bills to pay and accounting. We think in terms of vendors and accounting systems and all of those kinds of things.

It's a political entity. It is self-governing. You have the School Meeting and Judicial Committee, and if there's something that's happening that people are bothered by, they propose rules to control it. There's debate about what the best way is to deal with things, and people have differences of opinion and when they come to the School Meeting, people make arguments on all the different sides. You get to watch that whole process, and watch the way that, as the debate proceeds, people are undecided, and I generally find that there's a point where there's some kind of a critical mass sort of situation that happens and it shifts around to where you say, "Oh, I can predict the way that the vote's going to go now."

All of those things are fascinating, and they're all a microcosm of the world-at-large so you can see how so many things work in the world just by being here. That's what I like most about it.

Hanna: It's such a small school and one of the critiques that we get is that it's not ethnically or economically diverse enough. What's your answer to that?

Mikel: To me it's actually surprisingly economically diverse, given that the tuition is not insignificant. It's interesting to me the sacrifices people are willing to make to have their kids be here. Yes, there is a segment of people who aren't here because they could not come up with any way to pay the tuition.

Hanna: Does that bother you?

Mikel: The school reflects reality and I try to avoid being bothered by reality because there doesn't seem a lot of point in it. It is very much what it is, and that wishing it were something else is not productive.

Hanna: You sent your kids to this school. Were there any times that you were wondering if it was good for them to be here?

Mikel: No. I was very happy with the growth and development that they exhibited but I obviously had the advantage of being able to see that. They enjoyed school, they had good relationships with lots of people, people of all ages. They developed interests and pursued those interests. I thought they were turning out fine.

Hanna: I agree with you, that they turned out fine. But sometimes people have anxieties before the end point.

Mikel: I didn't.

Hanna: And your wife?

Mikel: She did not really either. As I said, to me when I first heard about this school, I said: that's exactly how a school should be. The picture of the school I had at that point is different than the picture of the school I have now, because I was really only seeing it through my own personal lens. This school for me would have been different than for a lot of kids who are here. I'm sure there are kids here who see it very much the way that I did, but probably not the majority.

Hanna: Maybe every kid has a different school.

Mikel: I think every kid has a different school. I think that's very true. That's something I've gotten a broader appreciation of, watching the way that it works for so many kids.

Hanna: Are your kids happy that they were here?

Mikel: Well, they had different experiences over time. My daughter never really had any doubt, and still does not have any doubt. She married another kid from Sudbury Valley and she is committed to having her children go to school here. My son was more skeptical. I think it's in the nature of children to question their parents' convictions.

One of the things I've often said that makes it hard for kids to go to school here, is that it turns out that a lot of the parents at the school are somewhat socially nonconforming in some ways. I think that for a kid who is interested in conforming, having nonconforming parents is a burden. And I think that when your nonconforming parents send you to a nonconforming school, that compounds the burden and that you get tired of explaining to people that your school doesn't have grades and that you don't have a favorite subject or any of those other things. That's hard for a lot of kids. I think that there's a certain element of that for my kids in that I've never had a strong attraction to conventionally held wisdom. I've always been one for questioning that. I often find myself in family conversations starting off and saying, "Well, I'm somewhat skeptical about that," at which point my children just laugh at me and say, "Of course you are!"

Hanna: I can see them rolling their eyes.

Mikel: I think my son wondered how all of these people who are on board with the conventional, traditional education system could be wrong and my crackpot father be right. And he very much enjoyed his time at Sudbury Valley! But I think he always had that concern. It makes me often think of the Walt Disney movie, Pinocchio. Pinocchio was off on his way to school and the fox convinces him not to go to school, and instead they go to Pleasure Island where you can just do what you want all day, and it's great. They get to fight and break things and do all kinds of bad stuff. And what ends up happening is that they grow ears and a tail and they turn into donkeys and they are packed onto a ship and sent off to work in the salt mines.

So that's one of those things: I'm having a great time, but shouldn't I be doing the thing that everybody else says I should be doing? Am I somehow setting myself back?

Hanna: I think that the pressure of the society-at-large is very strong even for kids with families who don't buy the pressure; the pressure is still there. And if you have a kid who is more social or aware of the society-at-large, they will have a harder time.

Mikel: I think he was very much aware of what he had *not* learned at Sudbury Valley, and not at all aware of what he *had* learned.

Hanna: Why do you think that is?

Mikel: You take for granted the things you have around you all the time. He grew up in a place where he was not special for having skills and awarenesses—all the kids did. Isn't that the norm? All kids grow up like this. And it wasn't until he went out in the world and started working that he had a better idea of the world.

Hanna: I also think that, for some reason, the kids in this school are highly intelligent, by and large. It's very nice for the students to have such peers, so you have interesting conversations and you learn a lot from each other. You have the time to have these conversations and to be doing things, which I think it's a result of having time to think and to pursue your own goals.

Mikel: Well, that's what kids want to do. They really want to think and talk to other kids. When I was in school, that's what I wanted to do. The only reason I went to school was because that's where the other kids were, everything else I could just do with a book.

Hanna: Is it important to you that you're doing something that has a bigger meaning than everyday existence?

Mikel: Yes. I can't imagine a way that I could contribute to making a better world than making sure that this institution thrives. There is a quantum difference between people who have been allowed to take responsibility for themselves and have been respected all their lives, and people who have not. We have people who grow up feeling that they are building the world that they are living in, as opposed to accommodating themselves to one that somebody else is running for them.

Hanna: What about passing on the wisdom and the culture of the adults to children, which is what the basis of all coercive education is?

Mikel: To me, the wisdom that's really wisdom, is compelling. People have a natural desire to engage with the things that are truly of value in our culture. At least that's my belief. I think that in places where people have tried to keep others away from it, they beat down the doors, they figure out a way to get it.

Hanna: There are lots of things that you did with your children that are part of your culture—your family culture, your religious upbringing, or whatever. You did teach your children, for instance, to be polite, to be generous, all kinds of behavior to be a good person in society.

Mikel: I think that the reason that you teach it is pragmatic: that it will make their life easier. They are skills, and I'm very pro-skills. I like to learn them myself. I think that the more skills that you have, the more freedom that you have.

Hanna: I feel that when you look at each family, there's a certain culture of each family that you can discern.

Mikel: Yes, but that culture of the family is the set of assumptions that enables the family to operate smoothly. The protocols that you learn are fundamentally pragmatic, and the ethics that underlie them will become clear to a child in due course.

Hanna: Like respect your grandparents, even if they get on your nerves.

Mikel: That's true, but I think we don't need to focus on that. If we focus on other things, whatever is important in our culture, people will come around to respecting their elders.

For example, I talk to my kids about their grandparents, and coming to grips with their frustrations with their grandparents—about seeing them as human beings who have extensive experiences that shaped who they are. They're a mixture: there are some things about them that are wonderful and that they love, and other things they have much more trouble with. Nonetheless, those are the people that raised their parents, and their parents are the people who raised them. I think that the context will all fill in.

The training that you give a young child is not ethically based, to me anyway. When I am trying to teach my granddaughter to say "please" and "thank you", it's not because I believe that if I don't, she will go wrong. I think that she is a good person just the way that she is. It's just that learning those protocols will set her going down a road that will make her life easier, and that in time she will come to understand why.

Hanna: But if you have two children and one of them—the older one—is mean to the younger one, that's not okay.

Mikel: What you teach them is that if you behave in an openly mean way to other people, you're going to get negative feedback from the people around you. I think fundamentally you're starting off by teaching them protocols, and that the underlying ethics of those protocols they understand later.

Hanna: Do you think we're doing it as staff here?

Mikel: I think that we certainly have the opportunity to. We talk all the time about the staff doing modeling, and that the students watch us all the time. We have the opportunity to model behavior we would be proud of and we also have the opportunity to model behavior we would be less proud of.

Hanna: I'm going to ask you something different. We've done basically all the excursions together—Nickerson, skiing, overnights—and I have observed for myself that over the years we, as staff, are more relaxed and we almost never yell, even though sometimes we are under stress. And we have succeeded in developing a culture on the trips where the kids almost take it for granted that they have to do chores, they have to be responsible, they have to watch out for each other. We don't even discuss it anymore. But time after time, we turn to each other after a trip and say: did you lose your patience? No! And it's not like we're such saintly people.

Mikel: Well, no, it's notable when it happens.

Hanna: We would yell, if we got irritated enough.

Mikel: And we have. We can count the times that those things have happened.

Hanna: Exactly. So, to me, that's one of the sources of great pleasure, that we've succeeded in doing that, that we've created that kind of culture in the school. Is that important to you?

Mikel: Yes. I believe, fundamentally, that people want nothing more than to grow into adults who have a rich, deep understanding of what's going on around them, who are ethical, and who feel really integrated into their human life. And that I feel the way we try to do things here is to be as harmonious with that as we possibly can.

Hanna: One of the things that you once showed me from the kitchen window is two little girls playing and talking, and you said they are constantly negotiating their relationships. You love to watch that, right?

Mikel: Yes. People want the things they want, but at the same time they also want to have relationships with other people. When you have two kids and they say, "Let's go play," the first thing they want is to play with another kid. Then they say, "Let's be dogs," and one says. "I don't really want to be a dog, I'd rather be a princess." Then they say: okay, you be the princess and I'll be your dog. They've just negotiated a mutually acceptable situation. Then they'll play that for a little bit, and they'll stop and negotiate further, because most of the time they would rather play and not argue about things. On the other hand, one of the things that I really like about four-square, is that arguing about four-square is one of the important things about four-square. People use that arguing time to learn how to negotiate a different way, to build logical cases and to cite evidence and all of those things when they're trying to get their way. There are lots of different ways that people go about doing that. It's all about working the balance between getting what you want and being in a harmonious relationship with a whole group of other people who are trying to get what they want.

What we go back to over and over and over again is *respect.* When I'm dealing with somebody I have a hard time dealing with, it's much more important for me to remember to treat them respectfully. If I'm having a disagreement with someone with whom I don't have a good relationship, I find it really important to fall back on really making an effort to be as respectful as possible. That's the reminder to me. It's easy to be respectful to people we agree with and get along with, and it's a lot harder to be respectful to people that we don't get along with.

Hanna: That's one of the things you have to do here. Not only as staff, but the kids have to do that towards each other and towards the staff.

Mikel: It's an important life lesson.

Lauren Ligotti

"Here you can see when you're useful. If you put your mind and your energy towards certain tasks, you can see the outcome. I certainly don't like wasting my time, not being active, so I think that's why I love this job so much because every day is different."

Hanna: Lauren, you were enrolled at Sudbury Valley. Tell me about your experience as a student here.

Lauren: I was here for three years. I started when I was sixteen. I spent most of my time reading and talking with Hanna and Joanie. I took classes with both of them and with Mimsy. I also did Danny's history seminar. Then I started thinking about what I wanted to do with my future. I never thought that I'd be able to go to college, because when I was in public school, nobody ever thought much of me, so I just didn't think I had what it took, and I started planning other things to do. My sister went to college, my brother is a plumber, and my family never put pressure on me. Whatever I wanted to do was fine. So I decided, while I was still going to school here, that I would go to hairdressing school. I would come here during the day and then at night I would go to cosmetology school right on Route 9. I did that for about a year and a half until I graduated, after which I started working as a hairdresser at a local shop. Soon after that I graduated from Sudbury Valley, and I realized that I probably could go to college. So I started applying.

Hanna: How come you all of a sudden thought you could go to college?

Lauren: I never thought that I would graduate from high school. So once I finally had accomplishments under my belt, I felt alright, maybe I'll try college. I always liked reading psychology books, and I took the psychology class with you, so I thought maybe I would become a social worker or work in the field of psychology, and I knew I would need schooling for that. So my next step was to go to school.

Hanna: You didn't have any grades from high school. Was it hard to get into college?

Lauren: It wasn't hard for me. I always said it was lucky they had nothing to quantify me with because they needed an interview. They had to talk to me about why I wanted to go to their school, what I was going to pursue there, and why I thought I was going to do well.

Hanna: So what you're telling me is that the interview sold them on you?

Lauren: I think the interview did. I was nervous, but I felt confident because I'd been talking with people a lot. At Sudbury Valley, all I did really was have conversations and talk about what I wanted to do, what was the next step, or talk about the book that I was reading currently, or about current events. I knew I was going to be able to explain myself.

Hanna: What gave you confidence? You have no tests here, you have no evaluations.

Lauren: I actually wrote about it when I was graduating. I was coming here and I was starting to feel better and I was like: okay Mimsy, I want to take classes, I want to set up a schedule like a high school. She said: well, if you want to do math, I'll do math with you. I'm terrible at math. I was struggling with whatever basic things she was trying to teach me. And Danny comes into the room wanting to talk to Mimsy, and she said: I can't, I'm working with Lauren right now. He said to me: what are you doing? You hate math, I know you hate math, why are you in this room? I said: well, I need to do math, I need to do all this other stuff that everyone else is doing. He said: you don't need to. Why don't you go read a book? You love reading!

Hanna: Why did you want to do the math?

Lauren: I just wanted to be normal, that's why. I just wanted to be like everybody else. So I started reading. I think that gave me the confidence to finally say, ok, I don't need to do what everyone is doing. And then everything else just came naturally.

Hanna: And you took the SATs in order to get to college?

Lauren: I started working with her again when I wanted to study for the SATs. At that point I was more committed because I had a goal in mind.

Hanna: Did you do well?

Lauren: Average. I had a friend that went to public school and I always thought she was so smart, and she and I got similar grades. Mine was actually a little higher. She's like, how did you get that—you don't even go to school?

Hanna: So now you graduated from high school, you finished cosmetology school, you actually got a job, and you applied and got into college. When did you get to do the hairdressing?

Lauren: Nights and weekends. During the day I would fit my schedule for my classes to make sure I was able to work.

Hanna: Did you have trouble with taking tests?

Lauren: No. I'm really good at memorizing things. That was never an issue.

Hanna: And writing papers?

Lauren: My sister helped me a lot with writing papers. She would edit them, cut things out when I'd start babbling on and on. She'd say: "nope, nope, no."

Hanna: You did extremely well in college. Did that increase your confidence or did you expect that would happen?

Lauren: I guess I never really thought about it. I was not planning to get a bad grade, that was for sure. You spend so much money to be there, you have a goal in mind—why would you waste your time? That's how I think I thought about it. I was the student that went to professor's hours and talked with the professor if I was having trouble in any subject. Usually it was math or science.

Hanna: Did other students do that?

Lauren: No, and in fact I always thought it was weird that they weren't. They want you to go there. I encouraged a few of my friends to come with me when I was going but they wouldn't have done it if it weren't for me. It was probably because of school here. Probably just being at Sudbury Valley makes you realize that the teachers are just people, there's no real authority and they want to help you through that subject. They want you to do well. And then there's another, probably psychological, thing where when they see your face and you're going there now you feel like you owe it to them to do better too. So you study a little bit harder, you can't waste their time.

Hanna: So it was a good experience for you.

Lauren: I liked college. I liked the books that they gave me. I remember students would always complain about buying a book that was unneeded or not wanting to finish reading a book. I never felt burdened by that, I always liked the textbooks they chose. I picked psychology to study so I already liked learning about it. It never really felt hard for me, unless it was one of the general education courses that they make you take.

I graduated magna cum laude, and I happened to be with five other Sudbury Valley students at the same time. We had no idea that we were all graduating. I met a few of them at graduation day. So that was exciting. And we were all in the honors program, graduating together.

Hanna: How old were you when you graduated from college?

Lauren: Twenty-two.

Hanna: Then what did you do?

Lauren: I decided that I was going to work at a short-term in-patient facility for at-risk youths who are homicidal or suicidal. I was there for three months, and it totally drained me. It was really sad. There's a certain type of person who can deal with this, and it's not me. So I decided to work full-time as a hairdresser.

Hanna: And how was it being a hairdresser?

Lauren: I did well. I had fun. You talk to people. You end up with a clientele that has similar interests as you, so most of my clients were social workers or runners, athletes; they read the same books that I do. It's funny how you find them and then they always come back.

Hanna: Then what happened?

Lauren: I started hanging out with Debra Sadofsky. She moved back to this area. I had worked with her at a summer conference at Sudbury Valley. She was the head of the work crew, and I was a student working under her, and we got along. She ended up contacting me; she knew I lived in the area, and she said: I'm around, we should have dinner. So I said ok, sure. And we met and we had dinner a few times. She started saying, you should be staff, you should consider it. I said I always wanted to be staff. I loved going to school there and I loved the staff members that were there at the time. Then one thing led to another and Danny and Mimsy were contacting me. I was working at the hair salon at the time and I had Mondays off. So every Monday for several months I visited school. I was with the students, walking around, seeing what I thought about things, and I talked to some staff members who were leaving.

Hanna: So then you applied to be staff at the end of the year. What year is that?

Lauren: 2014. This is my fourth year as staff.

Hanna: Did the kids gave you respect, even though you were so young?

Lauren: Yeah. I'm so young, but to them I'm old. They just see me as another adult.

Hanna: Do you think that having been a student here is helpful to you as a staff member?

Lauren: I think it's helpful when I see older students here that come in from the same situation that I did, because they're in that place where they're so anxious that everyone's telling them that they need to do something so soon, and they need to rush and rush and figure it out. They're at that point and they realize, why am I rushing around? So they come to this school and they finally relax and figure out what they want to do and then they start going right back into what they hated—math, like me. I hated math.

Hanna: Why do they do that?

Lauren: Because they just want to be normal. They want to be like every other public school kid. When you're that age, you don't want to be different, you don't want to be an outlier sometimes. You just want to be unnoticed.

Hanna: So why not go back to public school then, if you want to be normal so much?

Lauren: I was certainly not going back. You want to be normal and do all these things that the other kids are doing, but you don't want to do them the way that they're doing it. I just wanted to do what my friends were doing and not have to talk about the weird school I was going to. Like, see: here, I am doing something.

Hanna: What do you see as your role here?

Lauren: I would say that I'm an added resource for the students when they need me. And I try to learn how this school functions—how the physical plant is kept up and things like that—for the school to keep going and keep thriving.

Hanna: And that is a meaningful experience for you?

Lauren: Well, I feel like if I were to compare it to the place that I was at before, I felt so helpless in that hospital that me being there was just a waste of time. But here you can see when you're useful. If you put your mind and your energy towards certain tasks, you can see the outcome. I certainly don't like wasting my time, not being active, so I think that's why I love this job so much because every day is different. There's always different tasks. You have the same meetings every week, every day—JC, School Meeting—but every time it's different. So it's always interesting.

I think it's great when kids are able to grow up here because you can see the difference in a student that's always been here—how confident they are—and then the difference between a student that came here at sixteen. I feel like I got a lot out of it too. I just think that there's a difference, the kids who come here young do not have that time like a sixteen-year-old does who has to adjust and let go of all the anxieties or pressures that were put on them. Whereas a kid that grew up here, he's never had to experience that.

Hanna: Do you feel that it is good to give kids so much freedom and responsibility?

Lauren: I think it builds their confidence to be able to feel like they want to learn something or do something new and then there are so many steps before they can actually do that task. For instance, a group of kids, with me, started the Hairdressing Corporation; they wanted to learn how to cut hair. Well, before we got to that point, they had to get money, they had to build a corporation, they had to come together and meet as a group of people. There's many other things that you can learn, and then you finally learn what you want to learn. It's a huge sense of accomplishment.

Hanna: How is it different to be staff than be a student?

Lauren: Well, I can't read my books on the lawn, like I used to. In fact, I don't think I've sat on the lawn once since I became a staff member. I literally would spend hours reading my books in the sunniest spot I could find. So I can't do that anymore. I think that's the main thing. You know, there's work to be done and I try to find it and do it.

Daniel Greenberg

"Have you ever had doubts about the viability of the concept?"

"No, not for a minute. Every passing year strengthened me. Nothing ever happened that cast the slightest doubt on the ability of children to find out what's best for them. A lot of things surprised me because I didn't have a clue how brilliant the human race is, as a species. I knew that children were curious. I had my own kids, but you think your own children are wonderful. But to see in case after case after case without exception, especially with the young kids, the incredible inventiveness, creativity—not just curiosity, but ability to make their own world—I didn't have the terminology then, but now I call it 'making their own models of reality'. They aren't fantasy worlds. They used fantasy in their play to practice model-building, but when they were actually dealing with life, they were creating their own socio-political theory, inter-active theory, and more. They were doing it unconsciously and naturally, because that's what the human species is biologically evolved to do. And the extent to which they are brilliant did not really come through to me for years."

Mimsy: Can you tell me what about your life presented you with even the idea of having an interest in education?[1]

---

[1]This interview was conducted over a series of five conversations during approximately two weeks.

Dan: Everything about my life was about education. I grew up in a family where my father's main interest was education. He was a professor of education of the Jewish Theological Seminary, and he wrote textbooks for young children, beginning textbooks for learning Hebrew. Teaching is at the heart of the Jewish tradition—"you shall teach your children". He taught me Bible, and then my brother taught me Bible, and my brother became a teacher. Teaching was in the genes.

Mimsy: And your parents taught you Hebrew, or it was just spoken in your house so they didn't have to teach it to you?

Dan: That was my mother tongue. They spoke Hebrew, they were in a small group of people in the United States in the '20s who had decided to revive the Hebrew language in the United States—that is, to revive its use as a living language since there was a movement to restore it in Palestine from the 1880s on. My father got interested in that in his teens, in the early 20th century. So he and a group of other people decided they would speak Hebrew. And he was one of the main supporters and founders of the first Hebrew summer camp in the country, to which my brother and I went.

When my parents got married, my mother actually didn't know Hebrew as a spoken language. She came from a religious home, and she could read it. Very shortly after they got married, she spent a year in Palestine learning Hebrew so she could raise her kids in Hebrew. Everybody thought that my parents had split shortly after their marriage, but actually it was a major commitment to raise their children in Hebrew.

Mimsy: When did you start going to school?

Dan: First grade. I remember the first day as if it was yesterday.

Mimsy: Was it a linguistic shock?

Dan: Oh, no. I spoke English just fine, because whatever nannies took care of us spoke English, and the kids on the block spoke English. I was totally comfortable in English.

I remember the very first day. I was sort of interested in the idea of going to school; it sounded sort of intriguing before I had ever started. And there we all were, the six-year-olds trooping into the William B. Mann School on the first day of school. I still remember there was one little girl who was so tense and upset about going to school that she threw up. That was something that we all took notice of!

Mimsy: Why do you think she threw up at the time?

Dan: Because she was sad to leave her parents and to come to school, that's what I thought.

Mimsy: Were you eager to go to school?

Dan: Indifferent. I had a fine life running around the neighborhood.

Mimsy: And your friends weren't off at school every day?

Dan: No. The only friends I had were kids who lived two doors away. And they were pretty much my age—brother and sister. I think the sister was a little older. We'd been playing together since we were all three or four. I got to make new friends at school.

Mimsy: So you grew up with the idea that education was extraordinarily important because it was important in your family, not just what your father did but in your family itself—it was very important that you be educated.

Dan: It was so important that it wasn't mentioned ever. It was just what everybody knew was going to happen: it was a good thing.

Mimsy: That's what I'm trying to figure out because if it was so important that nobody talked about it, how did you even know that it was a thing?

Dan: I never thought of a category labeled "education".

Mimsy: But did you think about what education was?

Dan: No. It's what you had, like breakfast, lunch and dinner. It's what you got, it's what happens to you between 9AM and 3PM when you're a kid.

Mimsy: I know that it's at school, but you were talking about being educated in the home also.

Dan: That's what I'm saying: it wasn't a category, "education". The home was like one big hothouse of education. It was ridiculous. Every dinner together consisted of vast discussions about all sorts of topics in which my father, sometimes my mother, mostly my father and my brother and any guests that we had participated and argued and debated and discussed—every angle of. That's something I just grew up with. Anything that comes up, you're interested in. And anything that comes up, you delve into and turn over and discuss and disagree about and have violent arguments about and so forth. I entered that fray very early myself, piping up and giving my two cents' worth. And there was no quarter given for age, so age mixing was not a concept, it was just a reality. We were all treated the same. My brother argued intensely when he was twelve or thirteen. He would argue with the same intensity as my father. My father was very proud of his ability to delve into ideas, and he never stopped talking in a fond way about his life as a debater in high school when debating with a debating team was the primary team in high school at the turn of the 20th century. It meant a lot to him to be able to examine an idea, turn it over and over and over again, like a dog with a bone, hold the position as strongly as you could, listen to the other arguments and try to refute them, or change your mind. I mean that just happened all the time. In the beginning I was not really up to it and I would be very upset because my father and brother debated me when I was six, seven or eight years old with the same intensity that they debated each other. I felt overwhelmed and sometimes I dove under the table, crying bitterly. They found that a source of great amusement. They never consoled me. My father would always say, "You'll know you've grown up when you stop crying." And he'd say that also when my brother would viciously tease me. That was our version of "a stiff upper lip", I guess.

Mimsy: Very stiff. So do you feel that your ability to hang on til death do you part in an argument comes from that?

Dan: That's what it was. All my life I've felt the same.

Mimsy: Were you always considering that you might have children?

Dan: Never thought of it. It was like, was I considering that I breathe, eat breakfast? No, you grew up, you got married, you had children.

Mimsy: So you grew up enough to leave home and go to Israel where you actually met someone very quickly that you wanted to marry. Were you thinking of reproducing?

Dan: No, I was thinking of somebody I wanted to spend the rest of my life with, and I knew instantly that this was the person.

Mimsy: Okay, did you think that spending the rest of your life included having children?

Dan: Of course. If you're going to marry somebody, you have children.

Mimsy: What for?

Dan: It's what everybody does. We're talking now of 1952, when everybody got married and had children. This is the '50s for heaven's sake.

Mimsy: Everyone didn't get married and have children. My parents had friends their age that got married and didn't have children.

Dan: Everyone in my generation talked about it. I read books about the spirit of the '50s, the Eisenhower years, everybody wants to climb the corporate ladder and all that stuff. There was a post-war kind of re-grouping of traditional life. And I was just part of that. It was just not questioned, we didn't talk about it. But Hanna and I did talk about how we wanted to raise our children. Hanna was less in a rush to have children, and we didn't have children until she reached the great advanced age of 26, but we got married much earlier.

Mimsy: So now you have children. What did you think you were going to do with them? What was different about the way you were planning to raise them from the way you were raised?

Dan: Night and day. We were always talking about children, how we were going to raise children, but it's funny—you can talk theoretically! It's like what we get at the school all the time. You can read books about the school, but the minute you experience it, you realize that it's qualitatively different from anything you could imagine when reading about it. There was no imagining it, no matter how much we talked about the kinds of things we'd like to do or how we'd like to raise them, the minute we had children everything changed. The whole world changed, and it was like: oh, my God, there's this incredible phenomenon of this new human being entering our lives that we have brought into this world, and we were very aware that we were responsible for him. The things we do with our kid can affect his whole life! We never really worried what our parents might think about this, but we knew that we didn't want to raise our kids the way we were raised. We knew that 100%.

Hanna and I had a lot of things in common, even though we grew up 7,000 miles apart and in totally different environments. One thing we had in common was that through our early youth, and right up to the time we met, we were very much unsupervised, unmonitored by our parents. Hanna was a street kid. That's one of the things I loved. She was outside all the time, she was an outdoors person. It turned out—which I didn't really know until after I'd known her for a while—that she hated school. She wasn't interested in school, she was wild, she was a free spirit. I was different in that respect, but I was outside all the time. I was never home. We never had homework back then, until you hit high school. By high school I was in New York and we'd moved out of Philadelphia. Life was full of free time. Long summers were free, afternoons were free, weekends were free. I never did anything with my parents, they never took me anywhere. We didn't go on expeditions, we didn't go to shows, we didn't go to playgrounds, or the equivalent of Disneyland. Never.

We never went anywhere. But I went on my own all over the place from the time I was ten or eleven. I used to take the trolley downtown, Sundays, to the Franklin Institute with all the experiments there. I'd go to the planetarium; I thought that was the coolest thing ever. I sledded in the park by the railroad tracks with other kids. We were outside all the time.

Mimsy: That's how children were supposed to be.

Dan: Yes, and we were. My parents had no idea where I was. And when I got a bicycle, my friend Lenny and I used to go riding in the afternoons and certainly all summer long, when I was not in summer camp. We bicycled for miles and miles all over the city alone, we had the best time, and my parents had no idea where we were.

So, that part of raising our own children was normal to us. We raised both Michael and Talya bilingually. Our kids were going to be free and we were not going to be hovering over them. And they were. The classic picture of that for me is when our oldest son, Michael, was about one. He loved to play with water. One day we had the inspiration of standing him up in our little apartment in New York in front of the sink and giving him all the pots and pans and just turning the water on. He would stand there for an hour and a half, absolutely as happy as could be, with every combination of playing with water you could think about. We just left him there, we didn't worry that he was going to fall off his chair, or he's going to drown in the sink or anything. But about when he was two or three, right when we left New York, we started thinking, "What are we going to do with this child?" Then suddenly what school really was really dawned on us and hit us hard, and we said, "No way, this is not what we're going to do to our children." That's when it started. We're not going to put them in a jail.

Mimsy: And then?

Dan: That was the '60s, so people were talking about education, and I don't know how we came across it, but we came across the book *Summerhill*. For us, *Summerhill* was a tremendous relief; that somebody else had already thought about education, thought about freedom for children. We read the book, consumed it, and said, "Okay, this is the idea we want for our kids." We weren't subtle about it, we hadn't looked deeply into it, and it turned out later on that the model we ourselves came up with was inspired by Summerhill, no question about it, but certainly very, very different from the actual school. We read into it what our hopes and wishes were. So we started looking for a school like that.

At that time, because it was the '60s, there was a Summerhill offshoot boarding school in upstate New York and we got in touch with them. We weren't going to send him to a boarding school but maybe we could figure out some way to make it work that we live up there. Part of the Summerhill theory was that parents are absolutely the enemy. It's not just that they weren't to be involved in running the school, they were the enemy. Parents destroy children. A. S. Neill conceived of and ran Summerhill; he was a psychologist, and part of what he did every single week was have a psychology session—a therapy session—with each individual student. He called them "private lessons". He spent a lot of time on that. He believed that to free a child, you had to make that child not only feel independent of the parents, but also realize how awful his parents were. Anyway, we wrote that school in upstate New York. They basically said get lost, we're not interested in you.

Mimsy: Because . . .

Dan: I don't remember why but I'm sure we made it clear that we wanted to live there—not in the school but to live nearby. We weren't going to send our kid to a boarding school. And the idea was met with: no thanks.

Mimsy: They were taking five- and six-year-olds in boarding school?

Dan: That's right. That school closed, failed. And the man who ran it became a very embittered man and he actually moved from upstate New York to somewhere in the south. But before he moved, he came and visited SVS one day and he was just one big mass of angered bitterness at the world—and the fact that here we have a school that is inspired by Summerhill and is still running and succeeding while his school failed; somehow that meant we were awful people. We couldn't be more eager to get rid of him when he visited.

Then we went to see another school which was supposedly modeled after Summerhill somewhere in upstate New York. And we just walked in the door.

Mimsy: Did you have a car?

Dan: I had a car when I was sixteen. From then on I always had a car.

Mimsy: Where'd you get it?

Dan: From a used car dealer who my father knew. So we drove around, we were looking for schools and we came across this school—I forget its name. We walked in the door and there was a big open entry room and there were sofas all over and there were about ten or fifteen teenagers all stoned lying around on the sofas.

Mimsy: How did you know they were stoned? You know nothing about being stoned.

Dan: This is the '60s. I knew that a bunch of people zonked out who could barely see straight were not drunk. So I knew enough about drugs at that time. I couldn't have told you which drug necessarily, but it was clear as hell that they did not feel that there was anything amiss about an outfit where people were just lying around. I mean this is the era when it was actually respectable. There was Timothy O'Leary saying LSD was wonderful, everybody should try it. So it just wasn't our cup of tea, to put it mildly. Neither of us were interested in substances that altered our consciousness. So that was out.

I even went to the one Summerhill-inspired school that actually stayed alive for quite a few years—Orson Bean's school (The Fifteenth Street School) in downtown New York. Orson Bean was a famous actor and he got inspired and said, "I'm going to start a school." So he started a Summerhill school in Manhattan. At that time I was on the faculty of Columbia, and I went down and said to him, "I'm really interested in this, I'm thinking of this for our kids, and I would like to volunteer. I'll do anything, I'll sweep floors, I don't care. I would just like to see the school and experience it and be part of it." He looked at me and he said, "Do you have a teacher's license?" And I said: no. So he said, "Well, if you want to have anything to do with this school, go back, get a Master's degree in teaching from Columbia's Teachers College and then come back and talk to me." I thought: this guy must be kidding. My Ph.D. in physics isn't enough knowledge for you? I need a teacher's certificate? And this school is about *teachers*?

Mimsy: He was taking you seriously instead of the way you were taking yourself—I'll sweep the floors.

Dan: No. It was the notion that a teacher's certificate had anything to do with being a valuable member of a staff of the kind of school that I was interested in was so absurd that I knew that I never would want to set eyes on this guy again, and I didn't.

Mimsy: So that was it, that was all you could find.

Dan: Just think about our school, and realize that as far as many of us are concerned, one of the people who was central to the establishment and success of the school was Margaret Parra, who never went to college and who was from the Ozarks. She had tremendous life experience and wisdom beyond words and was "uneducated", and to think that you could even imagine that

A Gift

Celebrating our

50th Anniversary

~ SVS Press ~

her value was in any way diminished by her not having formal credentials was beyond a joke—it was pathetic.

Mimsy: Well, that is true but at the time that the school was starting you had a lot of people who had lots of formal education. So you really didn't have to sit around worrying are we going to be an intellectual enough group.

Dan: She was as smart as any of us.

Mimsy: No, she was smarter than most of us.

Dan: And as thoughtful. She could turn over ideas. In fact you can still see Margaret Parra in action in the wonderful film that was made as a Master's thesis by Paul Kelleher back in 1971 called "They Cry on Fridays". She's one of the people who appears in that film. And you get every bit of her wit and intelligence and sharpness if you see her in action in that film. She comes alive.

Mimsy: The group of people that started the school had plenty of people in it that were extremely intellectual and very able to come across as intellectual. Margaret, who was much more impressive and a lot more fun than most of them, was extremely brilliant and it was very easy for her to come across as somebody you really wanted to talk to and somebody who knew a lot. There was no question about that with her.

So take me from New York where you were thinking your children would probably have to be homeschooled, and I imagine you had never heard of that concept.

Dan: No, we did. We heard of the concept and we had actually talked about it. At that time we were very seriously beginning to consider making a school—we started thinking about that seriously in the fall of '65 already, when Michael was about four. But if we couldn't do that, we would rather send Michael to military school than homeschool him.

Mimsy: I used to say that about my kids too.

Dan: We just didn't want to have a child raised by us, with us hovering over him. It was worse than anything. In a military school, you know the enemy, and I always felt if you know the enemy, you can marshall your forces against it. Hanna knew the enemy, and school didn't affect her one iota. For her it was one big joke and she never related to it. A place with a known enemy seemed better than staying at home where your parents are loving you and caring for you and nurturing you and their asphyxiation of you is worse than anything.

Mimsy: I feel the same way about progressive schools actually— exactly the same way. And I always said I would never send my child to a place like that—that I would rather have them go to a military school. But I didn't really want them to go to a military school.

Dan: No, nor did we.

Mimsy: So what happened now? You're thinking maybe we'll have to do it ourselves, oh my God!

Dan: Yes, so we started thinking about that. At that time I was retired from the academic world, which I had left very, very eagerly, because I loathed it. It had all the worst aspects of the kind of schooling we were avoiding and no redeeming features as far as I'm concerned. And I've never changed my mind about that. I had a very nice advance from a book contract to write a textbook on introductory physics, so I could live for a few years without having a job that would bring in money. Hanna earned money as a post-doc in MIT so we were fine. We rented a house in Framingham Center.

Mimsy: You didn't find writing a textbook to be a little bit like selling your body?

Dan: Oh, no, for me it was fun, because I had figured out a completely different way to approach physics than all the standard textbooks. It was how I had been teaching it when I was in the physics department. I was having fun figuring it out—because I thought that textbooks were a joke, all of them. They were all the same, and I thought that their approach was wooden and really non-scientific. So I set out to write a different one. I drafted it over a period of several years, and I thought it was just a fun thing. I didn't feel as if I was contributing to the world of evil, I just figured: hey, it's keeping me alive and giving me an opportunity. The funny thing is, in the end it never got published because when it was sent to reviewers they said, "You should never print this because it's not like all the other books." That's literally what they said, I'm not making this up. So that was fine. I didn't have to give back the advance and I was very happy. I had time on my hands in addition to writing. I did a lot of reading and thinking about education. I drafted my first book on education during '66, which discussed some of my early ideas about how a school should be put together. They're certainly not Sudbury Valley, but they're not where I came from either.

Mimsy: What are they? Where is there a middle?

Dan: Most of it is pretty much like what finally emerged. But there were two basic things in that first draft that were wrong, two really core things in it that I had missed completely and really didn't understand until after we opened during the summer of 1968. I thought that there should be freedom for the kids to do anything—that I had clear in my mind. They should be free to do anything at all—fishing, walking, listening to music, whatever. But I thought that the school as an institution should be a resource center and therefore should have available not only a big library but also available classes that you didn't have to go to, but at least, if you wanted that kind of a resource, it would be there. This is pre-internet, pre- the ability to instantly get information from places. If you wanted to learn something about a subject, you'd have to go to a good library to get good books. So I figured well, if you really wanted a school to be a place where the kids had the opportunity to do what they wanted and find out what they wanted, it all had to be there either in the form of a library or in the form of people who knew about it and who were willing to talk about their respective fields. So that led to the "smorgasbord" idea—no pressure, no guidance, but the offerings are there.

Mimsy: That was basically the idea the school started with.

Dan: The school started with that in our test summer.

The other big difference was that the staff was seen as the major players. So they were sort of a self-perpetuating body in that original model. The staff were the ones who selected new staff members, the staff were the ones who did the administration and presented all the smorgasbord of courses. And I called them "the permanent members of the community", even though I was totally against tenure. They were not to be given tenure, but they were the ones who were there sort of long-term, whereas you expected students, "the transient members of the community", to come and get their education and move on and to have a life. It was expected that the students would come and go, whereas with the staff, if they were good and useful, they might stay a long time. I didn't really have the picture of self-governance clearly. I had the connection with the ideals on which this country was founded—life, liberty and the pursuit of happiness—but I didn't quite have the idea of who "consent of the governed" applied to totally. Because it seemed to me that it was not clear that one should give the vote to a body of people who you know are going to leave. Does Pennsylvania give the vote to students who were going to stay for four years and then move on?

That book was called *Education in Transition* and from that I produced a short position paper, which I wanted people to see.

Mimsy: Who?

Dan: Well, we started organizing meetings in '66 with a bunch of people who met in our house. And we had a really critical meeting at our house in '67. At that meeting the question was: do we open with a small core group of founders who were people that we knew—some of them were my former students from New York who had grown up and were interested in these ideas because I had been talking about them in New York in my classes a bit. Do we open this to anybody or do we keep it closed and self-perpetuate? That was sort of the test of the idea right there. The day of that meeting, by the most amazing coincidence, Fred Newman showed up—somebody who afterwards I got to know pretty well, along with his sidekick, Lois Holtzman. He had heard about this thing happening, I don't remember how. He was from New York and he was going to be a professor of philosophy at the time in a new branch of the State University of New York on Long Island. He was on his way from wherever it was that he lived to Long Island and apparently had passed through this area so he stopped by our house.

Mimsy: Wait a minute, you're in Framingham.

Dan: No, by that time I was in Sudbury. We had just moved into Sudbury.

Mimsy: In Sudbury? You need a crystal gazer to find your house!

Dan: He was probably somewhere in New England—I don't know, Vermont, New Hampshire—I don't know where he was before that. Anyway, he was literally on his way—talk about amazing coincidences—

Mimsy: And you had never heard from him.

Dan: Never heard of him, from him, nothing.

Mimsy: Someone in that room must have heard of him?

Dan: Never. We didn't know him. It was most bizarre. We were sitting in our meeting, in our house, and this car drove up outside, and out comes Fred Newman.

Mimsy: Was he weird looking?

Dan: No, he looked like a guy who was on his way to be a professor in a college. Totally normal. He got out of his car and asked if this was where I lived and he said he heard about this new school. I said: well, come in, we're having a meeting. He told me who he was, that he was a professor of philosophy and interested in political philosophy, and I said: come in, we're having this debate and maybe you have something to say. That's exactly what happened. He came in and it turned out later that when I got to know him really well, it was completely in line with his whole political philosophy. He actually ran for mayor of New York under a very radical ticket. He also founded a very interesting institute in New York for creative arts and everything—that's later. So he walked in and he listened to the arguments, and he said, "You have only one way to go that makes any sense and that is really compatible with what you're trying to do: open your doors, let anybody who wants to become involved as a founder come in and they'll self-filter. And the ones who are going to stay and be valuable will present themselves over time, but that way you won't be in a position of making these personal judgments. Instead, they will make themselves, and you'll get a much, much broader vision from this motley crew of people who will be attracted to the idea, but they'll all have their own interpretation of what the idea is." It was clear as day. He presented it, and we all said: of course. That was the turning point. How something like that happens in a person's life beats me, but it was a turning point.

*   *   *   *   *

Mimsy: Dan, there's something I want to ask you about. I personally also had children and raised them somehow, and came to some conclusions about what I should do with them as their lives unfolded, but before I had children I had never studied them, I had never thought about them. I don't even remember Mike and me talking very much about them, except I kept wondering during my first pregnancy whether I would still love them if they turned out to be stupid. I didn't actually realize that there was something else in the way of them being stupid besides the role of the dice. I eventually realized that I would like them fine, even if they were stupid. Then you have a child, and suddenly it's time to read the books about child rearing, and nothing any of them said helped me, nor did Spock: my mom had already figured out anything he said that was practical! So, yes, it's a totally life-changing experience. You can't go backwards on it, and it's not anything like you ever could have thought it would be. So was having a child anything you could have prepared for? Especially the child that you had!

Dan: Well, we didn't talk about the very specific having a child thing because we were married five years before we made the decision to have a child. So when we made that decision, we knew that part of that decision was how we were going to go about having a child. I don't mean the mechanics of getting pregnant, I mean what happens, what goes on, what is this about?

We also didn't have any real knowledge of children. This was the '60s so stuff was in the air, there were books that everybody read and talked about. That was when natural childbirth came into the big, big world of consciousness of our community.

Mimsy: Not mine.

Dan: Interestingly enough, Hanna's mother always told Hanna, "I had absolutely no problem having children, you guys were born like puppies." That left a deep psychological impression on her, and so for her the notion of natural childbirth was—of course, what else? I remember reading the books about this and that, and people going to Lamaze classes. So we read a lot about natural childbirth and how to prepare for it psychologically—both of us. There was some kind of group that she went to a few times and I think I went to once or twice, that also involved breastfeeding, which was absolutely not done in our highly intellectual circles. At that time, Hanna was still working on her Ph.D. in biochemistry at Columbia so she was connected to the medical school there. The hospital we were associated with was Columbia University Presbyterian Hospital, where the biochemistry department was, and the ob-gyn person there went along with the natural childbirth idea; wasn't totally enthusiastic about it, but did go along.

When she heard that Hanna was interested in breastfeeding, she thought it was just ridiculous. Hanna had to actually fight with her not to give her medication that would stop lactation, and also not to give her any kind of anesthesia or anything. So that's the way it all started. And we had a pediatrician who was dead against breastfeeding. It was all a battle, and the amazing thing is, we looked and looked and looked and looked during the pregnancy for books on breastfeeding—just to give pointers about problems you may encounter, like blocked ducts. There was not a single book available on breastfeeding, but we tracked down a book that was published in England by a veterinarian, who wrote on breastfeeding for humans based on her analysis of how animals fed their young. Just to give you an example of how ignorant everybody was: if you ask somebody about how it works, mechanically, most people would say it works on a vacuum principle, like you suck a straw; the baby sucks the nipple. There was no idea that the way you draw down milk from a nipple is by basically using the tongue to massage the milk out of the breast, rather than a vacuum drawing it. Sucking had nothing to do with how babies draw milk out of a breast, or how calves draw milk out of a breast, or ponies. She had all of the information: how she dealt with blocked ducts in cows, etc.

It sustained us, it got us through, because nobody else was ready to give us any support. And the minute anything happened, if there was the slightest thing wrong with Michael, we were told to stop breastfeeding. We went so far beyond what anybody thought was even remotely reasonable for breastfeeding. We went way beyond that and everybody was very upset with us.

Mimsy: So you were doing it on demand?

Dan: Well, we were certainly doing it on demand, but we were also doing it for months and months and months. There were people who said: well, if you have to breastfeed, six weeks, two months, that's it. Eventually, Michael stopped after about seven months and Talya probably a little longer. That was considered to be revolutionary.

We read Spock, who was totally revolutionary at the time because he was very permissive. For example, he took a very firm stand against toilet training. Everybody was potty-training kids, everybody. And you had to have your kid out of diapers by the age of one, or you were totally primitive, and certainly for bowel movements. The thought that it would go beyond one—well! Spock said no, no, no, just let them alone, they're going to grow up and they're going to figure it out. Don't worry, your kid will not get married in diapers. And he said there are kids who won't even get potty-trained until they're three years old. I remember the effect that that had on us because Michael, who was totally, totally in control of everything, just wasn't interested. One year passed, two passed, we're saying: well, three is coming up, and he'll certainly be potty-trained by three, and three came and went and then the day came when he was about three and several months old when we were scheduled to visit my parents in New York. Now, my mother was very, very priggish. We were very unhappy about the whole thing because we knew we were going to get nothing but trouble because Michael wasn't potty-trained yet, he was still in diapers, for God's sake, he's three plus! "What's going on with you people, you're a bunch of primitives!"—which they thought anyway. So we started packing and Michael said to us: "what are you packing?" And we said: "well, we're putting the diapers in," and he said, "Don't take diapers," because he was totally aware of my parents' attitude. We said, "What do you mean, don't take diapers? We don't need you to soil their sheets." He said, "I'm not going to have any accidents." Three plus, and he's having this conversation with us, and we said, "Are you kidding?" "No, no." Of course we packed some and of course he never had an accident ever. He could probably never have had an accident for a year and a half before that, but he just wasn't about to do it.

The other book we read was Gesell. The Gesell series of five books was very famous, and the parent of all of the curricula of today. It told you exactly every stage of development of the child and when it should occur. Those were *the* books. It covered things like the first month, the second month, the third month, the fourth month. People around us would freak out if their kid did not conform to the Gesell standards of when their kid was supposed to be at a certain place in their development, and they'd look for some way to fix things. So we read that, and we just thought it was absolutely garbage, and we never paid the slightest attention to it. At the time we thought it just didn't make any sense, and our kids had no relationship to any of these things anyway.

Mimsy: That's the thing: you have *real* children and they're not out of anybody's book.

Dan: Michael didn't talk at all, until very late, and once he started, he never stopped. For the longest time people would say: he doesn't talk yet, he's X years old. I don't remember when he started but he would sit there with his big eyes looking and taking in everything and not feeling like talking.

Anyway, that was our preparation for child rearing. By the time Michael was two and Talya was born, it was so clear to us that every kid is unique, has their own personality, is completely involved in finding out everything they can about the world and figuring out how the world works in their own peculiar way. It was just so obvious, it was not a discussion item.

Mimsy: So did the fact that you had babies extend for you into what you might think about schooling?

Dan: Well, we were thinking about schooling, but not about starting a school. We were doing what we wanted to continue doing. Exactly. The story that tells everything you have to know about that is that when Michael was about two, we had an outing to the Central Park Zoo. Now what kid doesn't like to go to a zoo and see animals? So we got off the bus at Central Park and there's a brick—not cobblestone, but brick—sidewalk that leads to the entryway to the zoo. And he gets down out of the bus, looks down, and he had never seen a brick sidewalk before because the sidewalks were concrete up around where we lived. He gets down on all fours and he starts studying it—looking at it, touching it, playing with it. We said: come on, Michael, let's go, there's the zoo right there, there's the door. He couldn't be less interested, he spent literally over an hour exploring that. He has never stopped, that's the way his photography is and everything he does. Every form interested him; that was it, and we knew then that if we mess with that, we're messing with the essence of his life.

Mimsy: Moving back to school planning. Fred Newman came and said, "Open it up," and then what? How did you do that? Who were the people in your group?

Dan: They were people we knew.

Mimsy: Were they really interested in starting a school?

Dan: Oh yes. One of them was Sandy Rabison, who became a staff member the first summer. He stayed with it the whole planning time. One of them was Steve Cooper, who then dropped out because he went to the Peace Corps, and his sister, Ina. There's a list of them in one of the very early pamphlets. These were people we had known and they knew about our theories and they were very interested. They were interesting people.

Mimsy: Was Dennis in there?

Dan: Dennis Flynn, absolutely. Dennis Flynn, who worked with me, who I knew from New York. David Chanoff joined eventually, but whether he was in that very first group I just don't know. But I knew him. I knew that he was studying at Brandeis University, so I invited him at some point. It was a small group, about six or seven people. We'd meet around once a month and I'd be writing and we'd be discussing things. We were going to do a PR campaign anyway, and that's when we decided to do some broadside publicity so we got in touch with groups that we thought might contain people who are interested. Where we were living was important to this. We had moved to Framingham.

Framingham was pretty diverse. It was still run like an old-time town with a power structure being in the hands of the WASP establishment who happened, most of them, to live in one tiny block in Framingham center called Warren Place, next to the Town Common, the Congregational Church and the Unitarian-Universalist Church. Right in that area lived the

State Senator from this area, and the physician who was like the town's physician to the north side. And there was his wife, who was the director of the Harvard Primate Lab, and also a member of the Framingham School Committee. And there was Harvey Ammerman, who was the pastor of the Congregational Church. And there was Fred Hilton, who was the town moderator and a lawyer in a Boston law firm. This was the power structure of Framingham, period, right there. And the next door neighbor to the barn that we had rented was the premier contractor for upscale homes, Mal Stalker, who opened up Salem End Rd. in Framingham and built all the luxury houses there. He was one of the sweetest people around, brilliant and down-to-earth. We didn't know; we just found this barn that was beautiful, and we rented it, and we were told by the owner that she had moved out permanently, but she didn't want to sell it, and we could stay there as long as we wanted. So we settled in and for these people we were like some kind of exhibit, an oddity, because they didn't know what to make of us. First of all, we were the first Jews that they ever really knew, and they were very clear about that. They weren't prejudiced or anything, it was just a curio. They treated us very well, they invited us over all the time, and we got to know them well.

So there we were; we were living our life, and we would interact a lot, and they knew that Hanna worked at MIT, and they knew about my connections. They called me "the Professor", and that was sort of their amusement. Then one day a turning point came when Mal Stalker came over and said his daughter, Bonnie, who was in middle school, and was having trouble with math, and could I just help her a little with math because he knew I was a professor. I thought: sure, why not, this would be fun. She was a darling; she babysat sometimes for us. So she came over and I helped her with her math, and she passed. Oddly enough, her first job was in the loan department of a bank! That gave me a reputation, literally, as: he's some teacher! That was my reputation in Warren Place, just from tutoring Bonnie, and getting her to pass middle school math. So when they heard that we were interested in starting a school, one and all they said they would support it. The Hiltons and the Randalls and the Johnsons all had school-aged kids. And they immediately were seriously considering backing the school, agreed to be members of the initial Board of Trustees, and helped us write the by-laws. They smoothed the way in town for us to do everything. They gave us advice on purchasing property, they drew up all the contracts, they wrote the by-laws, all pro-bono. Through them, the word spread. We knew somebody who was in the League of Women Voters—this was all in that era of ferment—so the word spread through them. I don't remember how we would announce the first meetings because where did you announce something? I don't know. But the very first big meeting happened when we moved from Framingham to Sudbury because the owner of our house had decided to return to her house after all. We bought a house in Sudbury. And I remember that first meeting. There were 100 people there. I actually have a tape recording of what was said. The place was mobbed, with all kinds of people. All very enthusiastic.

There was one key contact from that meeting, and that was Alan White—for many reasons. First of all, Alan White was at the time the principal of the Lilja Elementary School in Natick. He had been a math specialist teacher and then he became the principal of that school. He was known in the Natick school system as being somebody very interested in educational innovation. He heard about us, and because he heard that we were doing something innovative, his curiosity said: I want to see this. Another person that he was very interested in was Caleb Cattegno, who was instrumental in bringing Cuisinaire rods into America to help teach math. Alan was curious about all these new things, and he had some teachers from the school who came with him because they shared his curiosity. One of them was the librarian of his school and the other was Carolyn Low, who was a second grade teacher—lovely people. Also Priscilla Paris came through that Natick connection. Priscilla got very involved in the school, and in addition to everything else, she was a master typist. Priscilla helped us by typing all of our stuff, especially the biggest thing that we did: we sent out something like 120 letters to all the principals of all the area schools.

Mimsy: Personalized letters?

Dan: Yes. There were no copy machines or anything. This was when each letter had to be typed. They were long and verbose, as my letters would tend to be, and she typed them all. So somehow the existence of this experiment came to be known pretty widely.

Alan played a large role in helping people in the education world know that we were doing this. And then of course, we also connected with the '60s crew that was talking about "free schools". They came to know us, and a lot of those people would show up at our meetings, like John Holt who came and decided that we were great. He never came again, but later on, he had a different opinion of us. At that time he had written his book "How Children Fail" and he was a big name. I always thought there was something very strange because the same John Holt, who wrote "How Children Fail" and how all this traditional education is a farce, was an English teacher in the Commonwealth School in Boston! We would get the newsletter of the Commonwealth School and he would be writing articles that they asked him to write about how to teach English and this and that, and I thought: well, this is sort of interesting. Most people don't know anything about that side of him.

Then we started reaching out to newspapers. We got coverage with newspapers like *The Boston Phoenix* and another newspaper that went out of existence; they were underground papers at the time.

Mimsy: But not very underground because there weren't that many newspapers, and people actually were still hooked on papers because they had no choice.

Dan: So that's what was going on in that fermenting period of the fall of '67. We had been looking for a site before that. We found our site in the late fall of '67 and got the property, and drafted the bylaws, and we actually incorporated in February of '68. So a lot happened very quickly. But the gestation period began in 1965.

Mimsy: You had the site that you ended up with in '67?

Dan: We found it in '67. We had other sites already earlier in '67 that we lost.

Mimsy: Did you buy it? How was the mortgage being paid?

Dan: First of all of course, we had direct access to the banks because Bill Randall, the State Senator was on the board of one of the local banks. So what happened was Hanna and I put the down payment on this property. The property at the time cost $80,000, and we put down $20,000 and we took out a mortgage on the rest of it.

Mimsy: So you were having to pay this mortgage all along.

Dan: Yes, but very quickly, as soon as the school was actually a reality, we arranged to transfer the title to the school. That happened in the spring of '68.

Later we arranged financing with ten co-signers, and we got a second mortgage for the $20,000 we put in, so that the school would pay us back eventually, and our first mortgage was immediately transferred to Framingham Trust with ten co-signers. The co-signers were very well aware what that meant to the bank; they could hit any one of those ten for the whole amount if the school defaulted.

Mimsy: Meanwhile, who was paying the mortgage payments?

Dan: It must have happened close to when the first tuition came in for the first summer. That's the way things stayed until '70 when we desperately wanted to get ourselves out of the picture, because holding a second mortgage means you have leverage which we didn't want, and also to get the co-signers off, which Lee Chaplin, the President of Marlborough Savings Bank was willing to do.

He came and saw the school and said he thought it was okay. Generally banks don't want to give mortgages to schools because they don't want to have to foreclose. He said he'd take the risk for the bank and give us a mortgage with no co-signers, and we personally were able to get out of the picture. The bank never regretted this move because we were with that bank from 1972 until 2017.

Mimsy: They had nothing to regret.

Dan: That's the story of the formation. We had an enormous group of people who were going to be founders, and we worked with a bunch of them who got more and more interested in actually doing work. I guess the initial group who were ready to do work was somewhere around twenty. We decided we were going to open the school on July 1st, 1968, to give it a test run in the summer, and then start in earnest in September. There were a lot of people still on the staff in July.

There were a lot fewer when we opened the school in September; there were twelve. But in July there were quite a few more. And therein begins another tale because on March 1st, when we were absolutely certain that we were going to have the school available, we met and we said we're going to get the school ready for July 1st and we're opening, period. We told as many people in as many forums as we could find but we didn't have a single student at that point, except our children—not one. And when we opened our doors in July there were 130 kids, and a mass of professors from universities in the Boston area who all flocked to this wonderful place where they volunteered to give smorgasbord classes. That brings us to the scene when the school opens.

Mimsy: The school opened, and I wasn't there in July, just a quirk of personal circumstances. I came back August first, and enrolled my kids, so I didn't see a lot of what happened the first weeks. I saw a lot of what happened in the meetings previous to starting. They were pretty exciting, but what I don't quite understand is how this large group of interested people sort of condensed itself.

Dan: We kept having meetings—that was the key—we kept announcing meetings. The more you had meetings, the more people didn't come. It's that simple, really. By the time we opened, and we still said anybody who wants to can help us. The people who worked hardest were maybe the fifteen to twenty people who ended up being the initial staff.

Mimsy: Who were they?

Dan: Well, they were the twelve initial staff that ended up being there in the fall, and then there was some others, which I'll talk about because one of them was a big player there, Fran Ciampa, but there were a few others like that too. The initial staff were people like Hanna, you and me, then there were Joan Rubin, Joan's sister Myrna, and Luann Nathan and Marj Wilson. There was another friend of Joan's who was very much like Joan. Then there were Michael Dusenberry, Jan McDaniel joined. David Chanoff may have been in the original staff. Dennis Flynn certainly was, he was a major player there, and he became a central figure in the fall.

Then there was Jack Braunig, the painter, who became the resident in the building, to watch the building, and who we'll tell about later perhaps. Sandy Rabison was there also in July, but he disappeared early.

And Margaret, of course. Margaret Parra.

Mimsy: What caused Margaret to decide to do this?

Dan: We got to know Margaret personally because I was writing a book, I was working from home, and occasionally I'd have to travel. And Hanna was working full-time at MIT. We had two children, so we were looking for a nanny. We put an ad in the paper for a babysitter. Hanna was interviewing them. Out of the blue, Margaret answered the ad. It did not take very long in the interview for Hanna to realize that this woman is somebody we really wanted to have. So she was our babysitter basically for over two years, from the fall of '65 til school opened. She was just everything you could possibly dream in a babysitter, and the kids, Michael and Talya, worshiped her.

Mimsy: I think every kid who ever met her worshiped her actually. The whole gamut of people.

Dan: She was so life-wise, it was unbelievable. Her husband was in the Navy. He had worked his way up from the lowest rank. He was of Portugese origin from New Bedford, and he enlisted in the Navy and was in the peace time military in the late '20s and '30s, which is remarkable because the military was tiny then. He worked his way up to become a Lieutenant Commander and had the command of a destroyer. She would go with him to his various postings. One of the postings, for example, was a long posting in China so she lived in the Yangtze River area, but she had been all over the world. And she understood the whole point, you didn't have to give her a lecture, she understood what multi-culturalism was about, she understood what other cultures were. She could be amused by them and sympathetic to them at the same time. She loved human beings, and she didn't mind her own foibles and the foibles of the people she loved. This was pure. And salty. AND she could out-curse any sailor. She smoked, so she got right in with the kids who did—back then almost everybody cool smoked.

Mimsy: So it didn't bother you that she smoked in your house?

Dan: No. People smoked, they smoked in houses. My father was dead against smoking. My mother was insanely against smoking, she would take a fit, which is why I started smoking of course, because she was against it. But my father would say, "All I can say is, I don't know that it's harmful, but there's no way that putting smoke in your lungs could be beneficial." That was his way of looking at things, because he was not very sympathetic to the benefits you get from the effect of having this nicotine high. That didn't mean anything to him.

Hanna made me stop because she didn't like the smell, but to return to Margaret, she was good at everything. She was a great cook, but she was not only a great cook, she was a cook in a way that made the kids love the kitchen. The kids loved being with her—our kids when they were small. And she was just so much fun and so interesting, and she had more stories and more salty tales and more knowledge of the world than anybody I've ever met. So there it is.

Mimsy: How come she decided she wanted to be on the staff?

Dan: Oh, my God, she understood the school better than we did.

Mimsy: That doesn't mean she wanted to do it.

Dan: She jumped.

Mimsy: She worked her ass off here.

Dan: Oh, she jumped at it. She knew this was unique and the opportunity of a lifetime. She was so happy to be part of the school. It wasn't even a question. She didn't get paid any more than we did, which was not at all, at least for all the years she worked here. Her husband had a pension and he had a good job. He was quite an interesting guy in his own right. We got very close to them. There was never any question for her. All the meetings, the organizational meetings in the early days, she knew everything that was going on and she understood what we were doing, and she thought it was right on. For her, it wasn't a big theoretical thing. For her, it was the most obvious thing in the world, because she knew that the stuff that was going on in regular schools was the most pointless, worthless nonsense there is. Also she knew how smart her husband was, and he was just an ordinary guy who grew up without college and university education, and he was very successful and very well thought of in the Navy. So for her, schooling and paper credentials were meaningless. Character was what counted. She had character.

Mimsy: She sure did. Character **is** what counts.

Let's take you down a different street for a minute. I want to know something. In 1970, '68, '72, somewhere along there, if someone asked you what you did for a living, which people always do—I mean obviously it was working in the school. But what did you say? What do you do? What's your field? What would you have said?

Dan: That's two very different questions. If they would have asked what's my field, what do I do, I would have just talked about the school. I would have just said I'm involved in starting a new school. In fact, the Physics Association of America published a magazine at that time, and one month they ran an issue of what physicists who left the academic world are doing these days, out of the blue of random physicists. And they had a piece on me, that

I left Columbia and I became involved in starting this new experimental school. So that's what I would have said—I'm starting an experimental school, I'm working in the experimental school, helping it succeed, whatever.

How do I make a living? I would have said: none of your damn business.

Mimsy: It really isn't anybody's business. But you were employed very full-time at a school, so that's sort of the question. So somebody says: are you retired? Do you still work? And you say: yeah. Then what do you do?

Dan: What do I say? I'm a staff member at Sudbury Valley School.

Mimsy: "What does that mean? Are you a teacher?"

Dan: No.

Mimsy: "What are you?"

Dan: It's a very, very radical different kind of a school, and I am one of the people that the community hires to serve their needs.

Mimsy: And what if you have to put one word in a blank on a form, what do you write?

Dan: The forms that you fill out? Of course you say "teacher".

Mimsy: Why? I never say teacher.

Dan: Sometimes I may say administrator, but none of them are meaningful. Who cares? I mean they want to know what I do because they want to put me in a box. And they have this handful of boxes. We get these forms all the time and I have never understood who the insane person was who made these forms up. For instance, a form that asks every year to break down the school population by ethnicity, and has a list of 40 or 50 ethnicities like Chinese, Japanese, Korean, Caucasian, and I'm thinking to myself who could have made up this list because there is no person alive practically who doesn't have in his bloodline just going back three or four generations at least 2 or 3 or 4, some 6 or 7, different ethnicities. My father's father and mother were Ukranian, my mother's father and mother were Lithuanian, my mother and father I guess were a mix of Ukranian and Lithuanian. Hanna's mother was Russian, Hanna's father was German. So our children are Ukranian, Lithuanian, Russian, German. What ethnicity should we put down when we put down our children?

There's no meaning to these boxes. Nobody looks at the boxes except when they're making some kind of ridiculous statistical analysis, so what do I put down? I put down what they want to hear. Are you the janitor? If I put down "staff", they assume I'm the "janitor". Since I'm not talented enough to be a janitor, that would really be a lie. I can say "teacher" because at least if somebody pressed me, I could find something I could say I could legitimately teach. Not that I do, but at least I can.

* * * * *

Mimsy: I want to go back a little and ask you something— pre-founding, maybe even pre-1968. So a bunch of people met and some of them were more serious than others, some of them were destined to become staff, and some of them were destined to be staff for a second. There were people in that group whose input was very valuable. I know that no one's input is ever completely useless, because that's just the way it is, ideas come out of ferment, but were there people who were important to the development of ideas then?

Dan: Well, there was one person. Mimsy Sadofsky.

Mimsy: No, come on. I didn't ask you about her.

Dan: I've written about the contribution she made. Although, in its essential content, it looks as if it's a minor issue and I've written about it in *Announcing a New School*[2]. The contribution she made that had to do with the way our library was organized went far beyond the organization of the library and touched to the heart of what the school is about. And that was critical to everybody. There was an enormous debate over whether "children's" books should be marked with yellow tape. The idea was that younger children shouldn't be discouraged from reading by picking up a book that was too hard for them, which could ruin their appetite for reading. That was the standard librarian approach which Carol Shedd very articulately presented on the basis of a lot of experience as a librarian with little children. Mimsy was the standard-bearer for the other view, that yellow tags ran counter to everything we were about, which was treating children as people and letting them make their own minds up about whether they wanted to read any book. She made it clear that the idea that just because children find something difficult they immediately drop it because all they want is the easy way was absurd. And that's what it was really about. The question was: are children all about just taking the easy path the minute they see something, even though they're interested in it, and if it is a little hard, they'll drop it and never take it up again because it was so discouraging, which was the view behind that whole debate; or whether the approach we were taking is worth giving a shot. That's what was at stake. And we all knew it, and Mimsy knew it, and Carol Shedd knew it. So Mimsy's contribution here was not just about whether or not to mark books, it made us all think— the discussion made us all think. And her presentation of it was important. Other than that, I can't think of anybody—although I told you about Fred Newman which was a huge contribution.

---

[2]Greenberg, Daniel, "Announcing a New School", A Personal Account of the Beginnings of the Sudbury Valley School, Sudbury Valley School Press, Framingham, MA, 1973.

Mimsy: Yes, but it was a momentary contribution. Very important, with lasting effect.

Dan: Yes, it had lasting effect. I can't think of anything else pivotal. We talked about every little detail. A discussion raged about whether we should paint the doors to make them cheerful. And in fact the doors in our poor building were painted gaudy elementary school colors—yellow, red, blue. It wasn't until Hal Geddes came along, many years later, and had them dipped and the paint stripped, that they were returned to their original finish. It was a big process. Until then, the doors were jarring. But we didn't debate that, we sort of said well, it's cheerful, why not?

We didn't discuss things that later became issues—there were tons of them—but, for example, we didn't discuss whether the staff would be paid or not because we knew they wouldn't. Anybody who thought they were going to get paid the first year in a start-up was delusional. And we really didn't discuss, in the larger group, what the by-laws would be like, the legal stuff, or what the tuition would be.

Mimsy: Really. How did these things come about?

Dan: Eventually a core group filtered out that just did it; knew that there was X number of things to do and went through them—whoever the core group was. And there was a core group, which I talked about, of about a dozen people, who would meet very regularly and just assign these things to people to draft, or do it together.

Mimsy: What I am gleaning from what you're saying was that the real beginnings that never changed—working out the philosophy of the school—did not come from a group, it came from just a tiny number of people, probably you and Hanna, perhaps mostly Hanna.

Dan: It's funny, but I've been thinking about that since we started this, because the initial bylaws as legal documents to be filed with the Commonwealth, and on the basis of which our 501C3 was filed and all the rest of that stuff, did not mention the School Meeting. So if you look in those bylaws, you would have no idea that the School Meeting existed. And yet, everyone involved with the school, including the drafters of the bylaws, knew that the School Meeting was going to run the school. The bylaws had a few exceptions to it then. The document gave initial powers, that the lawyers felt was necessary at the time, to the Board of Trustees, and they gave some powers to the staff. But basically the lawyers, when they really heard and understood perfectly that the School Meeting was going to run the school, were shocked. Bill Randall paced back and forth and said, "four-year-olds voting, four-year-olds voting, Jesus Christ!" and he got all bent out of shape and thought it was insane. He was sure that they would vote to spend all the money on candy, that's literally what he said—the usual picture of children being nothing but selfish hedonists and not capable of any judgment whatsoever. So it wasn't in the bylaws at all.

It was only two years later, when one of our parents, Rene Gaillardetz, who totally understood the school, said this was crazy, we should not have bylaws that don't mention what the school is really about, we have to amend the bylaws. That's when the School Meeting came in. That made a huge contribution to the formal legal structure of the school, although it didn't change much substantial.

School Meetings back then were held on Monday, and on the very first Monday of the school, in July 1968, everybody got together in the barn and we had the first School Meeting. Everybody understood that this was the first meeting of the body that runs the school. And that's pretty remarkable when you think about it. There were no rules to start with.

Mimsy: As long as we're at the first School Meeting, what was the agenda like?

Dan: There was no agenda. The agenda was whatever we wanted to talk about.

Mimsy: What did people want to talk about?

Dan: Well, there must have been some things on the agenda. We have it in the archives. We have the minutes of every School Meeting. I know there were always agendas. There certainly weren't copies made of them for everybody to have at the very beginning, but they were posted. I think they were handwritten or typed, I don't really remember, but very quickly they became mimeographed.

Mimsy: What could have been on the agenda of the first meeting? Were there problems that had occurred already? Or were there things you needed organized?

Dan: I don't really know. I don't even remember saying that the meeting would be run according to any set of rules, at the time. We had to adopt the idea that they'd be run by Robert's Rules. But I think that may have been on the agenda—how we were going to run the meeting, who's going to be elected to be the chairman, that certainly was on the agenda.

Mimsy: Who the first chairman?

Dan: Well, I was. I just got up there and said, "Let's start and then select the chairman." And there wasn't any set term or anything. I guess things like that were discussed, like do we need any rules? I don't remember the very first rules. But I remember that very early on, the school was messy and we wanted to make a rule that you shouldn't litter. Jack Braunig was very much against that and thought it was ridiculous to make a rule like that. He said it's not such a big deal. And he proposed the rule: "let them that litter, litter; let them that pick up, pick up". And that was a rule in our lawbook until it was finally rescinded and replaced by no littering. That took a while.

Mimsy: So here we are back with the founding group. None of these people had ideas that molded the school, particularly?

Dan: Joan and Luann and Marj were very active in getting together stuff—like outfitting the art room, outfitting the playroom, there was a lot of activity.

Mimsy: But that's not really what I'm asking about.

Dan: That's not ideas, no, I know. Everyone seemed to be all on board. We talked stuff out at meetings over and over again. And everybody seemed to be clearly on the same page. We weren't aware until the big split in October, that some people saw this school so differently than we did. We just weren't aware of it. And I don't think anybody was.

Mimsy: It's funny, learning about the principles behind the school didn't seem that hard. It feels like it must have been harder to come up with than I think, but one of the first things I learned that had to do with working together as a school, and as a team of staff, happened I think in the summer, or very early fall, staff meeting. Someone, I think it was you, was complaining about certain rather routine work just not happening, like the doors not being locked at night or something rather large, I forget what it was. And you made a statement that I wish I could paraphrase, but that has stayed with me in every way. People were saying: oh, that's not my job, I did this, I did that. And you said, basically, all the work is everybody's job, that's the only way we're ever going to do this. I instantly understood and believed it—not that I did all the work, but I felt that that was an important thing for me to learn. It wasn't that I was a slack-off, but it was different, it was suddenly: oh, you really have to be conscious of everything, and everybody does. And of course, not everybody ever was, but it was a really big thing.

Dan: That's interesting because to me it seemed, as you say, just a given.

Mimsy: It should have been just a given but you remember that it was not just a given.

Dan: Oh, I remember! I remember the summer served a very big function, which I write about in *Announcing A New School*. There was the split in the staff in the summer, which happily preceded and played out in advance of the fall, when there was the split in the school body. But there are scenes that stand out in that summer, especially one of Fran Ciampa screaming at me in a big public meeting, "You have no love!" That was quite a scene.

Mimsy: I guess she got your number.

Dan: She got my number.

Mimsy: It's funny I have this in my list of things that I wanted to ask you about: everything is your job. How did you know? That is what I was going to ask you. How did you know that and what did it mean to you? Did it mean the same thing to you as it did to me?

Dan: That's such an interesting question. I'll bet you it's connected with my Israel experience—that's the way the country was founded.

Mimsy: Oh, of course, that's a pilgrim thing.

Dan: Everybody knew it. They formed cooperative settlements and there wasn't any question that everyone has to do whatever has to be done, it was in the culture there. I don't think I encountered that before, I really don't. But I do know something that we haven't talked about, and that's almost never talked about. I do know, now that you mention it—it didn't occur to me til now—there was something that occurred parallel to the school but definitely affected the approach to things. A subgroup of us formed, and Alan White was actually a significant figure in that group, because among other things I didn't mention was that he was himself a builder. He did that when he was a student in the summers to earn his tuition money and his living money. He would build houses with other people. He was a carpenter, and also knew all the trades, and understood architecture and knew how to do many things. He became better and better all his life and ultimately quit the world of traditional education and became a developer and a builder. But a bunch of us had read about the new fad that was developed in Denmark called "co-housing". That was a big thing in the '60s. We thought it would be really cool—at the same time as the school, not as part of the school but at the same time, sort of in sync with it—to start a co-housing community. And we even were looking at land. We read about co-housing, but more important, we would have regular meetings about co-housing.

Mimsy: I was very much a part of this, and in my memory that didn't happen until about '70, '71.

Definitely. I was there.

Dan: We all wrote papers voluminously.

Mimsy: Yes. And also our daughters Talya and Debra ever so often to this day say, "Thank you for not making us live in a co-housing community!"

Dan: The two projects fed off each other, in the sense of how do people work together, how do they cooperate, how do they build something new. We knew we were building more than just a place where you give classes; we were building a community for children and adults where they would grow together.

If we had made co-housing work, everybody would somehow have been involved in everybody else's business and judging everybody. I was very opposed to that part of community. But nevertheless, we put a lot of effort into thinking how people can work together and live together in harmony and make decisions together.

Mimsy: I think one of the things that happened was that it was too impossible to get agreement on anything that had to do with total living—anything. From special eco-friendly toilets to recycle human waste to anything one can imagine.

I know what I thought the school was going to be, and it turned not to be quite like a pastoral scene of meetings under trees, but I expected students to want a lot of wisdom and help from the grownups on a very regular basis, which they never really wanted that regularly anyway.

Dan: Two weeks into the summer I figured it out. I'm glad you mentioned pastoral scenes under the trees and I don't think it's silly or an accident. No, we had this mass of people from town say: oh, we'd like to be volunteer academicians. This was such a red flag flying high up there that everybody came to—professors from various universities and colleges, quite a lot of them. Because they heard about the school and it was so "progressive". I think I mentioned to you that one of our first students was the son of the Dean of MIT, who was John F. Kennedy's science advisor—the first science advisor of a president ever—Jerome Wiesner. And I still remember his interview in our living room—he and his son and his wife.

Mimsy: Why were you interviewing them at that time in your living room when you already had a building?

Dan: This was in March. It was before the building was inhabited. But as summer approached, these people all came out in droves and everyone said: I'm going to volunteer because I'm happy to help children learn stuff. And so there was this big list of things posted on the bulletin board: at this hour, at that place, so-and-so is going to be talking about this and that and the other thing. Huge, this was my "smorgasbord". And boy, did we learn a lesson, fast! What happened was that the very first week, everybody was thrilled, it was so much fun, you'd go and they'd all be under trees, the weather was wonderful, some were on the porches, some were under this tree and that tree. And there would be a professor and there would be like ten or fifteen kids sitting under one tree with one professor, and it looked so wonderful. That was the first day, and the second day, and the third day. By the second week the trees were there, the professors were there, and the kids weren't, because they didn't want to do this stuff.

Mimsy: No, of course not.

Dan: They were not interested.

Mimsy: They had no idea what they wanted to do before they started, and then they noticed that they could do what they wanted.

Dan: That's right. And then, we became the target of intense anger and hatred. It was *our fault* that the kids weren't coming to the classes. We weren't doing anything to encourage them to get educated! Boy, did we learn a lesson, fast. That's what these people were after, and that prepared us for the big split in October, because that's what the dissident parents wanted then. They wanted a school where you could at the same time say "everybody has free choice" and then have the "free choice" involve choosing from the options that they thought ought to be offered. Alan saw that very clearly. Long before, Sandy Rabison had said, "I know what the school is about. In this school *you're supposed to do what you like* and in progressive schools *you're supposed to like what you do.*" And that was just very, very visible. We learned that very quickly. We got that out of our system. The professors all vanished with a lot of anger, and that anger later overflowed when the school split because all these academicians' kids and the families close to them—all of the intellectual elite from Cambridge and Boston—deserted the school. I describe that whole scene in *Announcing a New School* at some length. Soon after, John Holt, the great guru of child-centered education that everybody still reveres (even though they clearly haven't really read his books carefully), heard all this and felt ashamed that he had been telling people about this school and that they had gone here, and wrote the Trustees a letter saying that the Trustees have to get rid of Greenberg, quickly, immediately, because "even if ten percent of what I have heard about him is true, he's totally unfit to have anything to do with educating children." The letter made no impression on the Trustees, but it was interesting that this great guru wrote this letter without ever having set foot in the school itself, or thinking that he ought to verify what he heard.

Mimsy: Well, he heard it from the right people.

Dan: That's right. "Agreed truth" is what I call it.

Mimsy: So you were comfortable with the nonprogressive point of view?

Dan: Yes, but I didn't even realize how far it went until the fall. In the fall we still hadn't really abandoned the smorgasbord idea, totally. So we would allow people to post things on the bulletin board with really no expectations on our part, but we didn't realize for a while what such a posting meant.

Mimsy: It took many years.

Dan: I don't think it was many years. I know there was a transition. I don't remember when it happened, but we came to realize that we can't let staff do that and we were very doctrinaire about saying to students: if you want a class, you go organize it, and then if you want us, we'll come. That did make a huge difference. But we didn't realize for a while that this big smorgasbord of staff postings became "the curriculum"—that what it did was suggest to students that even though we don't force you to do it and we don't really care if you don't do it, but if you really care about education, this stuff is available and you probably should do it. That's what the message is, even if you don't say it's the message. And that became very clear. For example, we realized that Summerhill's vaunted claim that it doesn't encourage or point people in any direction had long since been abandoned, and they made it obvious that they're going to direct people into certain areas of learning, whether they wanted to or not. So that was a big thing, to really realize the full implication. It surfaced for me recently when I was studying all this stuff that's going on now with "unschooling." One unschooler has a site in which she spelled out the difference between what's a very popular phrase now, "child-centered education", and "child-led education". "Child-centered education" means that you care about the child, you look at what they're interested in, and you create the guidance and curriculum around their interests. "Child-led education" is horrible—this is what the site said. It means the child just decides for himself what he wants to learn, and that of course cannot happen.

Mimsy: You know, the funny thing is that can't happen. A child has to really decide for himself what he wants to *do*, not decide what he wants to *learn*. It's the wrong word, it's always the wrong word—"learn". Because I don't think children do very many things with the idea of learning, they do them with the idea of: this is what I want to do.

Dan: The idea that you can get what you need to prepare yourself for life by having the child lead the way is just abhorrent to people who do believe strongly in child-centered education, where you look to see what their strengths are and their interests are and then you guide them to fulfill them, as long as they're not too far out.

Mimsy: At some point when the school began, problems must have occurred. There must have been issues either between people or disputes of different kinds that needed to be settled. What would the School Meeting do about that?

Dan: Well, when the school started, from the very beginning in July and right through the fall, right until the end of the year 1968, we used the model that Summerhill uses to this day, which was that disputes were all dealt with on the floor of the School Meeting. That was part of the School Meeting. If somebody had a complaint against somebody, or somebody had a complaint that something happened, we brought it to the School Meeting. And it's very interesting when you read the book *Summerhill*, these are very quick decisions. They don't have anything remotely resembling what we do. Somebody says so-and-so did this, so-and-so did that, did you, didn't you, I think he did, let's vote on a sentence—

Mimsy: Actually, it's quicker than that. I've been in a school meeting in Summerhill. I think that unless someone makes a big objection, if somebody else accuses them of something, it's just sort of like they wouldn't have bothered accusing them unless it happened. It's really one, two, three: so-and-so says so-and-so did that, etc. The decision of the group is very fast. And it's not that the person doesn't have a chance to speak, but there's almost no reason to.

Dan: So we used that format. The whole concept of due process and a thorough investigation and all that just wasn't a part of it. And somehow we got through things in the fall, and then things came to a head when it became very clear during the big split in the school. The thing that really solidified the character of the school from then on happened in October of 1968.

Hanna and I weren't there when the thing started boiling. And the person who was taking responsibility for the school was Dennis Flynn, who among other things was felt to be a rather abrasive person. Not that I'm not abrasive, but next to him, I'm soft and sweet. He's brilliant, but he can be abrasive.

Anyway, we went away because we were exhausted. We were exhausted for many reasons, but in addition to everything else, in August of that year, we had to leave the school for a week when my parents got involved in a very serious automobile accident. Automobile accidents have played a role in my life. My mother was really critically injured. Both of my parents were passengers in the back seat in New York near Poughkeepsie, with a high school buddy of my father's driving, and he fell asleep at the wheel. He got sort of hypnotized and drove right into a tree at sixty miles an hour. My father was shook up, but my mother had so many things happen to her. She had to have bone surgery. She was in the hospital in Poughkeepsie, and I went right out there, and my brother came out there from Philadelphia, and we both stayed there for a week. We gave blood. It was bad.

That was exhausting—emotionally and physically. And then there was the exhaustion of setting up the school and starting the new semester, and we just said: okay, the school's here, we went through the summer, it's running, we've got a routine, we can go for a week or so to the Caribbean, we just have to get away and get a little rest. When we came back, the school was on the verge of explosion. And the main issue was that nobody gave a damn. It was chaos. It was absolutely chaos. It was just what the lawyers expected.

Mimsy: Except that instead of foolish little kids, it was mostly disrespectful teenagers.

Dan: This was the '60s. There was a huge drug problem. When we came back, we were rested and girded for battle. We got the lay of the land quickly. From day one of the fall, all the staff had meetings every night. Without that, we never would have survived. So we got together and said: we have to bring this to a head in the School Meeting. Dennis Flynn, with the help of the whole staff, drew up a list of the people—it turned out to be about 30 or 35 out of the 130—who were clearly deeply into drugs at school and affecting the environment of the school negatively. We brought it to the School Meeting. We said these people are destroying the culture of the school with drugs. It's illegal, we can't do illegal stuff at school. We have to discuss each one of these people, and you know who you are. It was an intensely emotional School Meeting. It lasted three consecutive days, two or more hours every day continuously for three days.

It might have been more than two, but it wasn't more than maybe three. We went down that list—every single one of the people. Under the original by-laws the School Meeting did not have the power to suspend, but we could recommend that the Trustees suspend. The Trustees met and accepted our recommendations. They didn't really know any reason not to. And we suspended them on votes. Every single person was debated, voted on. I think maybe a couple of people that we accused were not suspended, about 30 were suspended. And each person had a committee made up of a Trustee and a staff member. The Trustee who served on most committees was Alan. I know I served on a lot, but I wasn't the only one by a long shot. Every single one of these people was given an interview with a Trustee/Staff subcommittee and with their parents, then the decision was made. They were suspended and they had to come to the School Meeting and ask to be reinstated. But, in between, because this was such an upheaval, the school was closed for a week.

Mimsy: The school was closed for a week because the parents had a meeting and basically voted no confidence.

Dan: There was an October 26 meeting—all of that was written up in *Announcing a New School,* but the fact is that only two people out of the 30 wanted to be reinstated; the rest withdrew. And one of the two people who came back became the first non-staff School Meeting Chairman, Mark Flora. I'll never forget that person, because he came back, and he said: "I know I was wrong. When I was suspended I went to the Cape, and I walked up and down the beach for days and I looked at myself and I said: what I'm doing is not okay. I was very destructive to the school and I regret it, and I want to be a contributing member of the community." And he did become just that. He became a very good School Meeting Chairman.

That was pretty intense. After it all came back together in November, it became clear that we needed a judicial system.

Mimsy: But did it become clear because the School Meeting's work wasn't thought to have been good? It seemed to me at the time that School Meeting's work was very careful and very good.

Dan: Well, it was and it wasn't, because we didn't have real due process. We didn't have the witnesses, evaluate testimony, all that. We didn't have all the stuff that we now take for granted. And that meant re-examining what a fair judicial process was. I wrote a paper that was presented to the School Meeting, and it set up something. We needed to give it a name. And the name that Dennis Flynn suggested, which I didn't object to at all, was an appropriate name borrowed from the outside judicial system—the Grand Jury—because what a Grand Jury does is not decide guilt or innocence but decide on whether charges even should be made. The idea of the proposed process was to have two steps—one, an investigatory step determining whether there's grounds for charges, and then to bring the investigation to the School Meeting, which would vote on whether to charge or not, on the basis of a full investigative report. Then either the person could plead guilty to those charges right then and there or a trial was held.

Mimsy: Some School Meeting member had to make a motion to charge and also be willing to prosecute once the investigation had been reported to the School Meeting.

Dan: That's right. But, just like today, most all of the time people just pleaded guilty.

Mimsy: So it was actually called a Grand Jury?

Dan: No. There was a big debate and that was when one of the people who had come into the life of the school, Charles Gaines, a Trustee (who was a wonderful human being, an incredibly sensitive and beautiful man, and the pastor of the Unitarian Universalist Church), made a very significant contribution, which I want to mention. He came to some of our School Meetings because he was intrigued by the school, he thought the school was a fabulous idea. He said: I don't think "Grand Jury" is a good name for this, from the point of view of the health of the community. I think you should give it a name like "The Committee on School Affairs". And so it was called "The CSA", as it remained until about 1982, when the whole new JC system was put together. And we adopted that as its name, and the procedure I described.

I want to mention the contribution the pastor of the Unitarian Church—Charles Gaines—made while the school was closed. During that crisis, after the parents had their huge protest meeting, he said: "Look, everybody has paid the tuition of $700 for the year (which was really very low) and it is non-refundable. Offer them the money back, and the ones who aren't happy will go, I know that from experience. I know that's the way people work." And I remember Hanna and I saying, "That can't be; it's their children! What does it have to do with a refund? If you think your kids are not in a good place, you're not going to leave them there just because you have some money in it and you're not going to get it back—you're not going to make them suffer for a year." He said, "Mark my words—they'll all go happily if you do that and not give you any trouble." So we talked about it and we did it, and they all left peaceably! A lot of the ones who left went and formed another school called the Satya School. It lasted for about a year or two and then vanished into thin air. That idea was a big contribution because we never would have thought of that, and we never would have dreamt that a parent would leave their kid in a school that they didn't think was right. And there it was—it worked.

Mimsy: Explain more about the CSA, because it was an investigatory body that was extremely, carefully set up with a lot of checks and balances I would say.

Dan: Well, it was set up really very much like the JC of today. The basic idea of having an investigative body where due process was followed, where all the witnesses were heard, where the committee met with five students; selected by age and picked by lot—that was definitely there. Everybody sat and discussed what they thought happened, interviewed witnesses and heard their testimony, and then filed a report with the School Meeting for the agenda. When the School Meeting met, it read the report and decided whether it wanted to charge anyone with a rule violation. The reports never came with a recommendation for a charge. The investigation and charging were completely separated so that one wouldn't affect the other. And the problem with the system was, even though it worked fine for twelve years or so, there was always a long delay between the incident and the end of it, because the incident would happen, the CSA would carefully investigate before they filed the report, and then it wasn't until the next School Meeting that the report would be published.

Mimsy: If you were lucky, because every witness had to be carefully interviewed.

Dan: And so by that time, it wasn't fresh in any way, shape or form. And that was hard, that was a problem. That problem was solved by doing something that is different from the outside court system that the Committee on School Affairs was mimicking, which was the transformation of the CSA into the Judicial Committee. In about 1981 or so, the planning started to happen. Scott Gray was very active in that as a student—Scott Gray and his friend, Tom Whalen, and Eric Draper—very active in writing the new charter and the essence of the new procedure.

David Chanoff was also very much a spearhead of it. In the end the big difference was that instead of waiting for the School Meeting to charge, after the investigation, the same group that did the investigation decided on the charge. And that is not that different from what happens in the outside world when the Attorney General does an investigation, and then decide on charges (or not). You still have the option that you have in the outside world of either pleading guilty or going to trial. There have been big trials over the years. In most cases people plead guilty if they think they are and get it over with, as is true in the outside world.

Mimsy: Have you ever, from the beginning until now, had doubts about the viability of the Sudbury school concept?

Dan: No, not for a minute. If anything, every passing year strengthened me. There was never any question that the idea made sense. Nothing ever happened that cast the slightest doubt on the ability of children to find out what's best for them. And if anything, there are a lot of things that surprised me because I didn't have a clue—I wasn't dealing with young children before then—I didn't have a clue how brilliant the human race is, as a species. I really didn't. I really had to come to that understanding. I knew that children were curious. I had my own kids and I knew what a two-year-old and a one-year-old was like and I knew they were all over the place. You think highly of your own children, and you think they are wonderful. But to see in case after case after case without exception, especially with the young kids, to see the incredible inventiveness, creativity—not just curiosity, but ability to make their own world—I didn't have the terminology then, but now I call it "making their own models of reality", and make them *real* models of reality. They weren't fantasy worlds. Yes, they used fantasy in their play, to practice model-building, no question about that, but when they were actually dealing with life, they were creating their own socio-political theory, interactive theory, and more. They were doing it unconsciously and naturally, because that's what the human species is biologically evolved to do. And the extent to which they are brilliant did not really come through to me for years.

Mimsy: You knew they were capable. I actually feel the same way and it shocks me that I feel that way, because I also knew that they were capable but I didn't know that they were brilliant. I didn't think about it for the first many years. And then one day about 25 or so years ago I realized that I was the dumbest "kid" in the school.

Dan: We never stopped digging and digging into this. It took the passage of quite a few years for me to understand, for example, the nature of language. And only after you understand the nature of language do you understand the unbelievable, monumental task of language formation that children do, on their own. And if there's nobody around them speaking a language, as everybody knows, they create their own. The very concept of language—the very concept of creating groups of events or things and noticing similarities, and labeling the similarities with a word symbol—is just mind-blowing. I became a little more sophisticated, and studied the nature of language and the philosophy of language, and I started reading Plato and Aristotle about what language is. I understood that they were coping with the same problems, because I never really understood before what they meant with their dialogues. I never understood what the whole Plato conundrum was about. Socrates, of course, made mincemeat out of definitions, and I always thought: oh, he's so clever! That's how it was treated in all the books. Socrates showed how inadequate any definition was, but they never really get to the heart of why that's so, why no word can be defined. Plato is struggling with it, but instead of understanding what a word is, he gives up and says it *must* mean something.

Mimsy: You'll never get there. You can only approach it.

Dan: You will never get there. So those are the kinds of things that took a lot of time. And once you realize about language formation, once you've gotten that, you realize there are so many other areas. My son, Michael, wrote this incredible essay, maybe 20 years ago, which is a long time after the formation of the school, in which he just says in a simple sentence: the three things that every human community has always done, no matter where they are or what they are: conversation, decoration, and music. Suddenly, it's the most obvious thing in the world. But where do you see that in the textbooks of anthropology? They don't say it that way, they don't understand that it is built into the evolutionary structure of the human being. They see it as sort of quaint, cultural commonality. But it's actually in the evolutionary human being. This is what they are, and who knows what evolution will bring next? Maybe it'll bring an animal that does something else too. But those three things that we do are not things shared by other animals. Animals don't make word symbols because they don't have self-reflection and self-awareness, which you need to make word symbols. As far as we know they don't compose symphonies or songs. If you give a chimpanzee a paintbrush he'll do something and you'll be able to sell it for $100,000. But you don't see them creating complex art on their own. So these are tremendous things, but it took me years and years to understand them. Once you understand it, then you go into the art room, and you look at a four-year-old sitting and doing things and you say: *this is real.* This is a person taking colors and pencils and stuff and making their representation of reality. The reason impressionism was such a big thing was for the first time artists openly said: we're going to put on a canvas what we feel we're seeing—not a direct representational picture of it. And that's what kids do all the time. And they've always been doing it. After impressionism came in, it became legitimate. Before, when children did it, they were trained to do better, and to be more representational.

So, there are tremendous differences in the way I see things now and the way I saw things 50 years ago. But they're all wonderful differences, and they just confirm what I now realize was based on not that much of a deep theoretical background. I had reasons to think that this was viable and real. I scribbled a lot. But every year brings new insight—to this day. It never stops. You learn things about the role of humor, you learn things about difference, about *real* diversity. For me, the difference between us and what's become a traditional education is just around that; suddenly people have lost the notion that no two people are alike. That's the nature of the beast. There's no standard model.

It's not like a car factory, that if you put a Ford out that has three doors instead of four because one of them is missing, then it's got a "disability", it's got a "door disability". It's like those things are so clear. But they *were* sort of clear when I grew up. In my school, people were just *different*.

Here's what hit home with me about that subject; how much ingrained it is in the culture of the school. And this is how it hit home. Something that never happened in any other environment that I'd been in is that you have kids who went to our school, and they're always able to connect with each other later in life if they want to. Always. Kids who have been friends in the school, it doesn't make any difference what they do, they still can remain friends. They still respect each other as talented, valuable people. So a kid can be a plumber, a kid can be operating heavy machinery, a kid can be an artist, a kid can be a jazz musician, a business man, a professor, whatever. They'll meet, they're *people*, they're friends, they'll talk to each other. They don't say: "Oh, hi, I'm professor so-and-so, what do you do? Oh, isn't that nice, you're a plumber." In my former world, you wouldn't even talk to plumbers! That brought home this ability of kids in our school to simply see other people as people who are whole and have their own genius, their own spark. That's the important thing—not what the spark is, but *to have it*. If you have it, you're my brother. And if you go to Sudbury Valley, the likelihood is you'll have it.

We also learned very quickly after the first year that you can't change the world—that the influences and the baggage that people come with are huge and that the later the kids come to the school, the harder it is for them to shed the baggage. But miracle after miracle takes place every year where many people are good at shedding the baggage more quickly and more thoroughly than others. We see people flourishing—some of them as if they had been there from when they were little kids, even though they may come at the age of thirteen, fourteen, fifteen.

Mimsy: It's interesting, I had a little thing like that happen the other day. An alum, who I'm in touch with personally, and is the cousin of two other alums who were in the school longer than she was and are both wonderful people, said to me, "I understand that your daughter offered to take in the cat belonging to the mother of the other two people til a permanent home was found for her. What a wonderful thing, you must be so proud to have such a wonderful daughter." She said, "I don't even know her," because she didn't interact with her at all at school, but it wouldn't have made any difference because it would have been just the same. They do it for each other. And they still do it for each other. And it doesn't make any difference how old they are or what the difference is, they have this certain level of trust: oh, you're the kind of person I went to school with and you're a real good example of it, and that's all I have to know. That's all in the world I have to know.

$$* \quad * \quad * \quad * \quad *$$

Mimsy: I asked you earlier if you ever had any doubts about Sudbury concept of schooling in the last fifty years. You said that you had not, but I also wondered did your children have doubts and how did that manifest itself, or affect you?

Dan: Well, it's hard to tell. Each of my children was different. I'm sure that Michael never had doubts. Being Michael, all he wanted was the freedom that he got here, and he's never looked back. Every time he talks about the school, his upbringing, or his education, he is totally grateful for it. Talya, being Talya, certainly went through her period of wondering when she was at school, and she and some friends of hers actually went to visit a public middle school. She was not enamored of it, but Talya was always uncomfortable with sticking out, with not being compatible with the mores of the ambient society. She certainly enjoyed her days at school, but she was very aware of the fact that it wasn't what everybody else was doing, especially since she was into skating and she met a lot of non-SVS kids at skating. And then she and her friends started taking dancing lessons.

Where did they have that little game of 1, 2, 3, 4, 5, 6, 7?

Mimsy: That was gymnastics. That was earlier maybe.

Dan: Gymnastics. There was all kinds of other things, and in all those places she met other kids. I'm sure most of them were very quick to inform her that she was stupid and didn't know anything because she didn't take regular classes. And probably they said the same things to the other kids of her group who went to these activities, so I think it stressed her. She was the only one of our three kids who went to college. She went to Weslyan, and she went to graduate school, and she got a degree and a profession, which she is very good at. She moved to Virginia so there wasn't any question of whether she would send her kids to a school like ours. I think that at some point, I don't know when, she realized what she had gotten out of the school, and she certainly has come to appreciate it and be grateful for it, and be grateful for the values she got from it, and she certainly has done everything one could ask for in a graduate, which is to carve out her own path, and become an entrepreneur really—several times over. So that's Talya.

And David was a staff member here for several years, and he worked to found and be a staff member at a school in Nova Scotia even while he was a full time farmer. So I don't think he ever had a doubt that this was a really first-class education. In my own immediate family, I'd say two out of three ain't bad.

Mimsy: That's sort of a fine thing to say—two out of three ain't bad, two out of three that never had doubts.

Dan: Yes, and the two boys would have been crushed in a regular school system, which would have tried to medicate both of them.

They'd both have been labeled ADHD, they both obviously can't concentrate on anything—which is sort of the joke of the year, which is, in my opinion, true of all ADHD people.

Mimsy: Yes, it is. So did that affect you at all that Talya was wondering if she was doing the right thing?

Dan: No, it didn't ever. She was Talya. You'd expect it. We were no more about to lead a traditional life style in general than walk to the moon. And she knew it, but she felt a little funny about it.

Mimsy: I'm going to ask you something odd, and I'm not sure you have an answer. I'm not even sure you'll understand the question because it's from a non-scientist. At some point your background in theoretical physics and history of physics, and your thoughts about education, sort of fused. Are you aware of that and how it happened?

Dan: Am I aware of it now? I certainly wasn't aware of it at the time. My intersection with history of physics came through an accident really. I was doing work in theoretical physics, and I did a paper with another person. I got interested in a certain aspect of relativistic physics which I don't want to go into. I started thinking about it a lot and it got me to thinking about certain basic parameters that are used in that theory. Every theory has space, time, mass, charge—basic concepts out of which they create their model of reality—and force, distance, all those things. And there was a particular set of parameters that interested me because they played a key role in relativistic theory and I started wondering about it and went to a colleague of mine who was a Nobel Laureate and I asked him something about it. He was a brilliant physicist, and his answer was: "oh, I don't bother about stuff like that, I start with a formula and go from there." There it was. Most of what he did was just that. He was good in mathematics and he started with certain givens and then he went from there and did some very imaginative and creative work.

That threw me for a loop. It ran so contrary to my way of doing things, which is always to burrow deeply into whatever it is I was doing, and it just struck me as being so weird. So I said to myself: okay, if he's not interested in it, I'm going to become interested in it. That forced me into what I've described as a journey back in history that I couldn't stop, because I said: well, where is this concept first mentioned? So I start at the beginning of the 20th century, and then I'm back a little further, and then before I knew it I was back with Isaac Newton and I'm thinking: wait a minute! I remember it vividly. I wasn't a historian of physics; I was always interested in history, and I knew how to do historical research, but I wasn't a historian of science. And there I am with Newton, and I'm seeing that Newton is playing with similar parameters, and at the same time I'm reading a book by a man who was at the time very famous—he's considered one of the founders of the academic field of history of science, George Sarton, a professor at Harvard. I think Harvard at the time was the only university that had a chair in the history of science. Sarton's books were very well-known. So I started looking this up, and one of the things that Sarton says, when he's discussing this with regard to Newton, is: really Newton didn't know what he was dealing with this concept, because when Newton uses it in his theory, his formulation is a tautology. And I'm thinking to myself: "Sarton, are you serious? Isaac Newton didn't recognize a tautology that *you* see?" The thing was so absurd, on the surface—that any person who calls himself a legitimate historian could have such a view, was just mind-blowing to me. I still remember my shock. And then I said: okay, but what was it for Newton? It was then that I discovered things about Newton that I never read anywhere. I hadn't read that much about Newton, but certainly if you said "Newton" to me, I would not have said: oh, yes, Newton, the famous chemist! But he was the most famous chemist of his day—back then it was called alchemist— but he spent most of his energy on that, most of which never saw the light of day later because people were embarrassed by it. He was looking for a way to turn materials into gold, and in the meantime doing top-rate chemistry, which is probably why he became the director of the mint in England!

That's how I got interested in the history of science. And once I got interested in the history of science, that was the beginning of the end for me of any kind of respect for the academic enterprise as it existed in my environment. I realized that there was something rotten in the state of Denmark, something really bad going on.

Mimsy: So wait a minute, you didn't stop at Newton?

Dan: No, I'm saying I went back to my long trip through time. Of course we had to find out where Newton got it from. I ended up with Aristotle, I ended up with pre-Socratic philosophers!

A colleague and I actually wrote a book on Anaxagoras, a pre-Socratic. That was another thing that affected me in my attitude towards academia, and towards the way things had been taught and done, because if you read the literature on these early philosophers, including Aristotle, you find people saying that Aristotle wasn't a scientist—for example, he gives the wrong number for the number of teeth in a horse's mouth. People said, "What kind of scientist writes about the teeth in a horses's mouth and gets the number wrong? He obviously didn't care about reality. He just wove these nonsensical theories!" But for a thousand years Aristotle was the gold standard of physics! After Newton, he wasn't anymore, so therefore he must have been an idiot. And I'm thinking to myself: I wonder how many people who write biology books or natural history books have actually counted the number of teeth in a horse? They ask somebody who has horses: how many teeth do they have? And if the guy gave him the wrong answer, he didn't say: did you count them? He assumed that the guy knew.

No one took these early people seriously. So we wrote a book called *Anaxagoras and the Birth of Physics*. We included "physics" in the name of the book because we realized that all the translations of these ancient people were gibberish. You could compare them to having Einstein translated from German by a German literature professor. The translator has no idea what he's writing. They translate the words and they don't take him seriously. But if you look at it and take him seriously, suddenly you realize: hey, this guy's a bonafide scientist talking about serious issues and coming up with some damn interesting theories—that's what our book was about.

By then I had reached pre-Socratic times—I was back in 500 BC and all illusions were gone about the worth of a standard education. Now did that connect directly? I didn't turn around during this trip down history lane and say: well, that means I've got to get involved in starting a new school for kids. No. But it laid the groundwork and made me a fertile ground for the seeds that dropped on me from reading *Summerhill*, because I had to think of schools, and so did Hanna, for our kids. And I knew I didn't want them to go to regular school. I didn't want them to be part of the regular system, but I wouldn't have thought of an alternative if I hadn't read John Holt and *Summerhill*, and stuff like that. The two together were just like the perfect storm: you don't want to fill kids with the accepted truths that the academicians have decided are reality—just avoid it, start from scratch, let them figure it out themselves. I don't know if that answers your question.

Mimsy: It doesn't really answer my question, but it's a very interesting answer that answers a question that I didn't ask. I don't know how to ask my question any better. You didn't want to take anybody else's established answers. You told me that, just now. You didn't tell me how that and education are one thing for you.

Dan: Well, I was a failure as a teacher. I was part of the establishment, and here I am teaching physics while I'm doing this research that eventually led me down the slide. I love physics—that's why I became a physicist. I had my own peculiar way of looking at it, which I developed on my own. I don't know where it came from. But anyway, it wasn't quirky or anything, it was just a different way of approaching how you teach physics, not the standard textbook way. I didn't turn my back on the standard progression of subjects, I still taught mechanics first and electricity second and then light. I didn't depart from that, although there's no good reason for that progression. But what I did do was try to explain things in a new way, instead of teaching the same way I was taught when I learned physics, to wit: these are the laws of physics, here's how you do it—this is distance, this is time, this is velocity, this is acceleration, F=MA, all this stuff that everybody did, which always got puzzled looks from everybody. I wanted to explain to them where all this stuff came from. They were thinking that these are truths that have come down from scientists, who were the same as God. I said to myself: it's not pedagogically a good way to do it. I wasn't thinking of anything deeper than that. The standard way seemed so arbitrary. I tried to tell them a little about how people who thought this stuff up were thinking, and that turned out to be a very original approach. I still don't understand why it isn't the standard, but it isn't, even to this day. So in order for me to get the lesson across about the physics I wanted to teach that day, I tried to figure out a way to get the material in that lesson to resonate with their minds, and the only way to do that is if they can sort of identify with the minds of the people who created the concepts in the first place. I didn't know the minds of those people, but I tried to imagine where these ideas came from and I'm mostly making it up. I'm not yet a historian but I'm thinking: let's see how I can make this sound reasonable.

Now, I can give a good show when I talk. I liven things up. And I'd be very enthusiastic about it because I was excited about this way of presenting stuff. So I'd come into the room, there'd be a classroom full of people. In that particular course, the first one I taught, most of them were pre-meds, or pre-somethings, and the last thing on earth they wanted to hear was physics. Physics majors were never a problem, you just threw the book at them, you say this is what physics is, learn it, suck it up. So I had a challenge. I'd come in every time with a new lesson plan, which I had thought through, and I'd present it with all my dynamic showmanship; often at the end of the lecture they'd clap. They loved the classes.

But they had a textbook. You cannot do it without a text-book with problems in it. And I'd give them tests, and none of the stuff that I taught ever went far enough to reach the test page. None. Ever. In the beginning, I thought I was dreaming—but *none of it*. It was like they went home, they looked through the book, they studied what the book said, they parroted it back. And I'm thinking: wait a minute, what's going on? And I kept working at it. By the second year, I was asking other people who taught physics for ideas. I'm thinking, what's wrong with my pedagogy? I've got all these ways of getting subject matter across, and they're listening and they're loving it—and it doesn't stick! I remember this vividly: by the end of the first year, I knew from my total experience, I felt it in my bones, you cannot get people to absorb subject matter unless they want to learn it—unless they're thirsting for it, in which case they can relate to you, if they want to hear you. If they don't want to hear you, nothing will help. But if they really want to learn the subject and they want to know what this guy thinks about it, then they'll listen, and they'll remember. Curiosity, interest, passion for the subject, and interest in hearing a point of view—that was clear to me. And all illusions about the value of pedagogy flew out the window. They didn't learn physics as far as I was concerned. They were parrots. It was clear to me. The subject matter that I made lively was the same subject matter, but you could detect quickly from the way they answered whether they were at all interested in my take. And they weren't, because they really weren't interested students; it had just been a good show.

Mimsy: But you didn't test them on what you thought physics was. They were interested in it when you were doing it.

Dan: No, they weren't. They were seeing a fun show, and they didn't relate it in their heads to the subject matter. That's my point. If I would have said: "okay, guys, this course is about my show, and after every show, I want you to tell me what the script was," then they would have done it. But somebody told them in the course description that it's about physics and that this is the textbook, so my show was like a sideshow.

It became so clear that when I was invited to become a professor of history, I told the administrators when I started: "I'm going to do it my way and I don't care whether you like it or not. If you don't like it, don't even have me, but I'm going to give my lectures and I'm not testing them, and I'm not giving them grades. End of sentence." It was hard for them, they didn't like that, but they were sort of stuck because there weren't a lot of professors of history of science. They wanted to start a department and they didn't have anybody to turn to at that time.

Then yesterday I remembered something that was a turning point in my life, as I realize now. We joke about how a former SVS student named Alex, when trying to get reinstated after an indefinite suspension, said "the old Alex is out the window, the new Alex is now going to start." I don't know if I ever told you this story. In the summer before my third year of teaching physics I was really sort of desperate. I have this scene in my mind's eyes so vividly: I was sitting at the table that I worked on. It was our dining room table, and we lived on the 21st floor of a high-rise building over the elevated railroad on Broadway and 124th Street. It was summer; we didn't have air conditioning so the windows were open—they were swing-open windows. So there I was sitting in front of the window, and I figured, alright I'm just going to prepare this course in advance so I don't have to think about it anymore. I was sort of discouraged. I was about three-quarters of the way through the whole course with my lesson plans—lesson by lesson by lesson—when a huge gust of wind came, and the entire pile of lesson plans flew out the window—21 stories high! I got up in horror, watched that whole mass of papers slowly floating down to the street. For a moment I said to myself: go down and try to get them, and then I realized that was ridiculous. Even if I could get ten or twenty sheets, there's traffic, etc.—it's gone.

I thought: fine, I'm not going to have lesson plans. But in a way it symbolized a deep change in me: in a real sense, the old went out the window—literally. That's it, no more of these lesson plans, no more anything. You've got to start from scratch and do something different. So I do think these things are all tied together.

Mimsy: Okay, almost answered. I still feel that your interests have melded more in the last few years—maybe five or ten—than ever before, but maybe not.

Dan: Melded in what sense? In the academic world?

Mimsy: No, in your mind.

Dan: Oh, to me, it's all one now. It took me a while to realize to what extent, but everything I've done in my life has drawn on every other thing. I mean that literally, as fields of endeavor.

Everything in my writing can be traced to every step in my life, very directly.

Mimsy: When you go into school now, how do you feel?

Dan: Elated.

Mimsy: Why?

Dan: It's funny. I'm going over an interview that a certain Hanna Greenberg made of a certain Mimsy Sadofsky. And the interviewer asks that very question, and both the interviewer and the interviewee on more than one occasion during this long interview use the word "elated", so I guess that's where I got the word, but it certainly represents how I feel.

I love getting to school and I love encountering the kids from the minute I get in—I don't care who they are. Just seeing them. The way they walk into school, and they're busy and they're involved and they basically either ignore you because they're too busy—but not in a rude way—or they greet you warmly. And you feel that you're in this living organism. The school is alive. You feel embraced by life. That's the only way I can put it. It is so exhilarating to be in that environment, even when you're dealing with big problems or you're angry at somebody or aggravated that somebody did something really stupid, or broke a rule and they really should have known better, whatever. It's the intensity of the interactions. I love intensity and I love the fact that people are strong and that they stand up to you. I don't always enjoy what they do, but I sure as hell enjoy the spunk, I really do. How can you not?

Mimsy: I enjoy it too, so you're preaching to the choir. Have there been times when you haven't felt that way coming to school on a regular basis?

Dan: Occasionally. There have been periods where there was tremendous divisiveness in the school. A period like that has not happened since the new bylaws were written. As long as the parents felt that they had some control over the way the school operates—and they did, legally, under the old bylaws, although they were never able to exercise that control—they never gave up trying. There were periods when they just kept trying. The first set of bylaws, as I mentioned before, didn't even mention the School Meeting, even though everybody knew it ran the school, and in every set of bylaws since then, until the final revision, the "Assembly" had less and less power, but they always had the fundamental power of setting school policies.

The point is, that meant that you were subject to this periodic sort of battering—it was like waves of little groups of parents. They were always a minority that were really determined to take over the school and guide it in a different direction. That often led to a very bitter atmosphere in the school. The kids were involved in a lot of these splits. The parents would stand in the parking lot, and it was as if conspiracies would be formed. They'd waylay people in the parking lot—other parents—and talk to them and plan how they were going to do this or do that in the annual Assembly meeting.

Mimsy: How do you know it's not still going on?

Dan: They don't have power. I don't care if they stand in the parking lot and talk about anything. The only power they have is to withdraw their kids. I always felt throughout the years that as far as I'm concerned, nobody's forcing you to like the school. If you don't like the way the school operates, then leave, that's okay. But why would you try to take it over from the people who are making it happen and have a philosophy and like what they're doing? It happened from the very first year when we had the big split.

Luckily the only reason the school even exists is one thing that I'll never forget, and Hanna will never forget. When we were writing the original bylaws, when it was the Assembly and the Trustees who had the legal power to do everything even though the School Meeting existed, the question was: did there have to be a residency period before somebody could vote? And we were democratic, it was the '60s, and I said: no, no, no, if you're there, you're a parent, you should be able to vote. After Hanna insisted on a residency period, Fred Hilton, who was the first president of the corporation and the lawyer who drew up the first set of bylaws with Bill Randall, who was the State Representative and also a lawyer, they were just insistent, agreed that it made sense to have a residency period. So Hanna prevailed. If that three month waiting period before getting a vote in the Assembly hadn't been there, there would have been no school, because the split happened—believe it or not—on October 26th, which is less than three months from when it opened, so they couldn't take over. They wanted to take the property. They couldn't do it, so they pulled half of the school out, they went to Lexington, they rented some property there, they founded the Satya School. And they were gone. They would have been even happier if they could have taken our school.

I don't expect all people to love us. Today, parents who don't like the school pull their kids out. It happens every year. And it's heartbreaking when it happens, especially with kids you get very close to and attached to. But they're not taking the school away, they're not trying to control us. They realize that is a non-starter because of the new bylaws. That's totally changed the atmosphere in the school, because before that you were just wondering, during these waves of dissidence, what was the end going to be. And they were ugly splits. Even now, when some parents leave the school, they're very ugly in what they say about it. But who really cares? I did care though when they were saying it right in the hall of the barn when we were in an Assembly meeting and they were trying to sway people and tell them how awful we are and that they should get rid of us.

Mimsy: When you think about Sudbury Valley in five, ten, fifteen years—each may be different—assuming that the world has not totally exploded, what do you think about as the future of our institution, or the theories it embodies?

Dan: I don't have any doubts: the theories are constantly getting refined, deepened, better understood, modified—but not changed. Because the theories are so tied as a whole. The way we deepen them is by seeing more and more facets of humanity, of the nature of human beings, of the human soul, and of the human spirit, that are compatible with this way of doing things. Evolution might create a new species and everything will be different. But assuming there's no evolutionary change in the species, we're on rock-solid foundation.

I feel that way not just about the school but about the country, because as far as I'm concerned, the country and the school are identical in their core values. I do think that the survival of the school and the flourishing of the school will be connected to the survival of the country—that I don't have any doubt about. And should the country abandon its unique approach to organizing society, one that no other culture has in the world has to this day, then I don't have much hope for the school, because then it will stick out like a sore thumb. But to the extent that the country feels that these core values are worth preserving, even if we were the only ones who do it, then the school and its ideas should thrive and get less and less hard to carry on.

I think that the school is going through a very difficult period now because the country is. The country is definitely going through a difficult period of whether or not we actually believe in the ideals that we said we believed in. I think that they will triumph, because they have been so deeply embedded for several hundred years, but there are pressures from the rest of the world for us to change, because the rest of the world doesn't buy these values. If the country can withstand it, we'll survive. If the country can't, I think there is little hope. You can see that because all the Sudbury schools that have been set up in the rest of the world cannot function as real Sudbury schools—anywhere, in any other country. And I would not be interested, for example, in being associated with a Sudbury school that has restrictions that are placed on it.

Mimsy: Well, I wouldn't be interested either, but if I had a choice of sending my child to public school or to a school that had a few restrictions, I don't think at that point I would choose a military academy. I think I would choose something with the ideals I liked and the inability to bring them all to fruition.

Dan: There's no such thing. We don't agree. I'm much more in favor of "know your enemy". Know that you hate your school; if you do, you'll survive it. Hanna hated school. She knew what she hated and it stood her in good stead. And I like that. I had to overcome the fact that I *didn't* hate school, but I had other things that helped me.

Mimsy: I wonder how you could not hate school. What was there to like?

Dan: It didn't affect me. It was nothing for me. I had so many outside interests.

Mimsy: But weren't you bored while you were in those hours at school?

Dan: For me, it was a game. You get a 100 in tests, it's sort of a game.

Mimsy: Why? It's a boring game, it's not worth playing.

Dan: I can't say. You know you have 50 minute periods, some of them are boring, but most of them were just like: huh, I wonder what this person's schtick is. And some of it I actually liked. I loved math, I loved physics. But English was totally boring. The books were horrible. I never read a book after that until I had to in college.

Mimsy: Yes, reading and writing are really drummed out of you in school, and arithmetic usually too.

Dan: Not for me.

Mimsy: No, not me either. The idea for these interviews was invented by, of course, Hanna. And she has done most of them. She couldn't do your interview because you seem to be married to her. So you're stuck with me. But we do have a lot to talk about and a lot in common so it hasn't been so bad. I am wondering— because I don't think we're ever going to have this kind of publication again—1967 was the last time I remember there being anything at all written about staff members. And I think this is going to be a powerful piece of writing in its totality. So I think that if there are things that you feel that you wish we had covered, or wish we had covered more, then this would be a nice time to talk about them.

Dan: We've never talked about building an institution and what that means. When the original founding group first started to discuss opening a school, one of the first things we were told was that you can't even think of founding a school if you don't have $250,000—this is 1967, so that was probably the equivalent of about $2,500,000 now. Their idea of a school of course had nothing to do with what we were going to do. What we had at our disposal was $40,000 total. The question is: what was going on in our minds to even think we could? I was very aware of what it meant to have an institution, and I think that's part of my background that we didn't talk about at all. This is where my father, and all of the rest of my background, come in and then all of the other skills that it takes, and all the people who have worked with us—especially you—that it takes to actually create the tremendously varied facets of an institution—a press, a PR campaign; this is a big enterprise for a little school.

Mimsy: It is, and when we first started talking about how the founders group got founded, and who was active in it, I was sort of fishing for that, I guess, and not really getting it. But I hadn't fished for it with the right words.

Dan: I guess the reality is—it probably sounds like this is bragging, but it actually isn't—that I was the only person with a direct understanding of what it takes to found an institution.

Mimsy: I'm sure you were.

Dan: And that's worth talking about.

* * * * *

Mimsy: Dan, in 1965, '66, '67, '68, probably '69, '70, there were tons of alternative schools. Where'd they go?

Dan: Into thin air.

Mimsy: Why?

Dan: I've often thought about that, and it really is only recently that I've begun to understand the answer to my satisfaction. The same question applies by the way not only to the myriad schools that began in the mid '60s into the early '70s, all of which disappeared, but also about the many Sudbury model schools or schools that were inspired by Sudbury Valley, the first of which started in 1991. Why have such a very high percentage of them disappeared, and yet they continue to be formed? I don't mean that they need to be modified, or that they disappear because of governmental requirements, which is universal in Europe and may have been a factor—I don't know that it ever has been—in some places in the United States. The answer that I gave, and I think it was the right one, with respect to the schools that disappeared in the '60s and '70s, was that they were like almost everything else that happened in that period. They were slipshod, they were seat-of-the-pants, they were created by people who had an idea, thought they would do it, were enthusiastic, and then moved on to something else.

There was always the same feeling: we're going to rent a storefront, and we're going to have a school; or we're going to have a bus and ride around the city and it will be a school of the city; etc. And there was so much of: we're going to have a democratic school, we're going to take votes, we'll do it all by the seat of our pants, and maybe we'll ask somebody for money, or we'll get grants, or we'll do it with no money, and everybody will love us, whatever. It was all love and enthusiasm and really an almost absolute absence of ideas. There were slogans: "democratic", "free"—it was called a "free school movement".

To me, a typical archetype of the kind of thing that would go on is John Holt, who is so revered to this day, because he wrote these books about how children fail and how children learn, and people were very excited about them. I was too when I read them. But then at the same time John Holt was employed at the Commonwealth School in Boston, which was a traditional prep school. He was an English teacher there. Somehow, for quite a while we got their bulletin, which was just like the bulletins of Buckingham, Browne and Nichols or Milton Academy or any of the other private schools, and there was always a piece by John Holt about how to teach English or how to teach this or that. And I'm thinking: there it is, right there. You can spin off a book very nicely about "this is what children need", and then you don't even walk the talk—your own talk, let alone anyone else's. So there was a shallowness in the movement that is almost unfair to the word "shallow". So that's my answer to that question.

But we would also puzzle about why Sudbury schools disappeared. It's a very different matter, because pretty much all the people who have started Sudbury schools are people who have taken some trouble to look at some of the literature. Many of them buy Planning Kits, which doesn't mean they read the contents, they might hope that they will osmose into their system by sitting on a desk. But still, they look at this stuff, they talk to other people in Sudbury schools, they see themselves as serious people trying to do a serious venture.

Yet, school after school fails, and really not a single one of them in the United States has reached the numbers that we reached from '86, '87 on. Why? I remember talking about it over and over, and we would say: it's because they didn't have enough committed staff. Many of them would have one or two or three founders. It's just too big of an enterprise to succeed long-term if you don't have enough committed people. We always had a lot of people on the staff, whether it was all full-time or full-time plus part-time, but we always had half a dozen or more. Right now we're operating with a smaller staff than I think at almost any other time in our history. I know we would talk about it and say: they just don't have enough staff, and those that they do have don't have the energy, or lack some other essential quality. It's only recently that I have reached a very different conclusion, and that's really what I want to talk about here.

I think the thing that brought home to me the need to reexamine the question is looking with a clear eye at our school today, fifty years on. The school today, in our 50th anniversary year, has seven staff members. We have three staff members who have been there from the beginning—three founders. And we have four other staff members who have come anywhere from 30+ years ago to this year. And you think about that and you say: wait a minute, let me think about that a little more. And I realized that in fact these three founders were the core group from the beginning through all the fifty years.

Mimsy: I wasn't really there at the beginning—in '67 for instance.

Dan: In your interview you say: I'm not a real founder, because I wasn't there. No, that's not fair. You were a founder, and anybody who lived through that long, dry period of struggle from 1968 to 1985 and functioned effectively qualifies as a founder. You were there essentially for the whole time. You were there during the formative period, you were there during all the struggling years, and you were out just for a couple of years when we did have a whole bunch of people who were sort of like the "free school" people—very enthusiastic and enjoying the ride, and they kept the ride going until you came back. But the fact of the matter is that the school's heart was those three founders. And no matter how hard we tried over the years to add, to enlarge that heart, to find others who were commensurate with them, we had not succeeded. It is only now that we are reaching the point where we can anticipate success.

That led me to think really hard about what it was all about. What did the three founders bring to this enterprise that made it different, that made it stand out? They gave it sustainability, viability and, much more to the point, it became possible exclusively through their efforts to make this more than one school—to make this something that is known all over the world. Our books are translated into many languages, schools have started all over the world that claim to be similar to us, or to be inspired by us, and education textbooks and courses all over the world discuss what we are doing.

What's going on here? How did it happen? What did the three founders bring to it that made this happen? It's never a question of numbers. I've talked about this a lot. Tiny groups are the ones that have always brought big change, I mean eensieweensie groups. A little tribe in the middle-eastern desert, a tribe of nomads wandering from the Mesopotamian Valley to Egypt and eventually to Palestine, created the whole universe of monotheistic religion and ethics. A tiny group of people in a handful of little city-states in Greece and Greek-speaking territories created the entire basis for Western culture. And then a small group of people who weren't highly educated, who were considered backwoodsmen by all cultured Europeans, who sat in a few colonies of the British in this wild, remote place across the ocean—that group became the Founding Fathers of the great American experiment.

There was something in each of these groups that sustained them and made them special. What was it that did that for us? It was easy for me to understand the special characteristics of the other two founders. Not all the characteristics, of course; you never know another person totally. But when you've worked with people for fifty years, and in my case lived with one of them for 65, you have some insights into them. It was easy for me to understand the factors at work in the other two. It took me a little longer to figure out what I brought to the table—as silly as that may sound. I'll turn to that shortly. But it was clear to me from the beginning that Hanna brought certain very specific kinds of strengths that were highly unusual—one of which was "in her mother's milk", so to speak, because her mother had them to a degree that was well-known throughout Israel: she has an affinity for people, for understanding people, for just "getting" people and being able as a result to relate to them on so many levels, with complete naturalness and ease, and furthermore across the spectrum of personalities. She had no hierarchical attitudes towards people, she didn't think that some people were better than others, that some people were worth more than others, depending on position or reputation or fame. For her, a person was a person. Her mother was exactly like that. Her mother could talk to a plumber or a street cleaner with the same ease that she could talk to the president of Israel, and in the same way, without awe in one case and without looking down in the other case. Hanna is exactly like that. As a result it has been amazingly easy for her to connect with parents and students across the spectrum and with potential staff and with people in general—including officials—no matter who they are. That was huge.

Another huge thing was that she had a lot of wisdom, and a lot of good instincts. Time and time again, she really saved us from going over a precipice, not by waving a flag and making speeches but by very gentle guidance. She is just extremely wise about how to handle people, and that's really important if you're trying to build an institution based on people, and especially children. I mean that's almost your major ingredient. Without that you don't have a school. You may have structures but you don't have inhabitants.

And it was very clear to me that you, Mimsy, brought a unique combination of many of Hanna's people skills in a completely different style, which was also good, because both of you relate to the full spectrum of people—kids, parents, officials, everybody—with the same ease but you do it with very different styles that are complementary. In those instances where the style of one of you may grate on somebody, the style of the other almost always comes to the rescue. So the spectrum of human interactions is really covered incredibly well between the two of you. And you also have the same basic set of skills that I bring to it, which meant that I wasn't working on my own, I wasn't working out of my own fantasies, out of my own imagination, my own intellectual structures. I always had somebody who was a peer to interact with me and build on what I was doing, critique what you and I were doing and help clarify stuff. Because God knows when you're creating a new structure based on new philosophical foundations that are constantly being refined and explored, if you don't have at least two minds, that are complementary, but are not in any way identical, working on it at the same intensity and depth, then you've lost something—you'll never get anywhere—you need that. Every one of the groups that I refer to—these tiny groups—always relied on the fact that they had variety in their thinking, and you didn't need more than some variety to do it.

So what did I bring to it? It's only been recently that I've even really asked myself questions along the lines of who am I, and what did I do? And I realized that institution-building is really about creating a culture and creating a place for the culture—creating a new social structure. Institution building was in my life stream from earliest times. First of all, I grew up during the period of the building of the Jewish homeland in Palestine. Every bit of that was part of our daily fare—at home, and in our discussion groups, in our youth movements. People talked about what it took to come to a country—a bunch of people none of whom really had any experience in this—and to build agricultural settlements, to build cities, to build an internal governing structure.

In 1947 the U.N. met and passed a resolution dividing Palestine into two pieces—an Arab piece and a Jewish piece The Jewish piece was in recognition of what the British had promised to Jews in the Balfour Declaration in 1917. The U.N. cut the country up and said: this is going to be the Jewish country and this is going to be the Arab country. Part of the Arab country was immediately conquered and taken over by Jordan. And another piece of the Arab country was taken by Egypt. But there was this central section which had been given to the Jews who had settled in Palestine. This happened in the late fall of 1947; and in May of 1948, Ben Gurion declared that a new state was going to be founded called "Israel".

What happened was that from the very earliest time, basically in the '20s, the Jewish settlers created what's called "a shadow government" to which they, by consent, related. It was called the Jewish Agency, and it had a central building in Jerusalem.

In the Jewish Agency, they developed over time all of the divisions and ministries that you'd have in a government, including defense and energy, a foreign department, everything. They were not an official government because they didn't actually govern anything. They were a voluntary organization set up by world Jewry, who had contributed funds to it. The local Jewry in the various settlements throughout Palestine participated in it, had people who served in it. There was no formal document empowering it. In an informal way it was recognized as the authority that speaks for the Jewish settlers. There were competing groups that thought that they might want to do things differently, but they were always a minority. Basically, the country was united.

So in that interim between the U.N. vote in '47 and the establishment of the State of Israel in 1948, they needed that shadow government, because the minute that the U.N. assembly had their vote, all the surrounding Arab countries invaded the Jewish territory in order to destroy it and take it over and throw out the Jews. The Jewish community fought to survive, and they succeeded. By May, Ben Gurion, who was the leader of the Jewish Agency, the shadow prime minister, had decided that they were stable enough, they had defended themselves to a satisfactory degree against seven Arab countries.

Mimsy: How could they have commanders in chief or commanders?

Dan: It was all done from that shadow government, it was all there, it was all in place. It had been in place—the Haganah, which was the name that their army was given, had been in existence from the '20s. It was totally organized—platoons, divisions, everything, armored tanks. They even had a little air force that was cobbled together very quickly at the end.

The point I'm making is that I grew up with that. To me, institution building was what you did. You create institutions, you create all the pieces of it, you have to put it all together. You have a picture of what you need. And these were things that I was aware of. We didn't sit around the table and say: how do you build an institution? It was in our everyday conversation; we talked about the various parts of it and came to understand almost from day one what it takes—the breadth, the vision, the integration of the various parts, the specialties that you needed. All of which had to be at top performance in order for the thing to work.

Added to that was the fact that my father was an institution builder many times over. First of all, he came to Philadelphia as a rabbi in 1925 to a brand new congregation that was just in formation. He was a young graduate of the Jewish Theological Seminary. There was a small group that said: we want to have a congregation. The Seminary sent them this young graduate, and he built a temple in the western part of Philadelphia, in Wynne-field. By the time he left it was considered one of the two or three premier congregations in the country—not just in size, but in richness of content. People would come to see it. It had a school, it had lots of functions going. It wasn't just a place where you had prayers and marriages and funerals. It was a place where you had vibrant adult activities, vibrant women's activities. The people there participated in national Jewish organizations. He had to get the money to run it. He had to run the school. He had to get a principal. He had to put all the pieces together. And of course this was table talk. We talked about this stuff. He would come home and talk about it with my mother, and I'd hear about it. I'd hear about the trouble he was having with the school principal, about what it took for him to build the library there and to find a librarian, or about the problem of finding a cantor so that the musical program could be okay. All these things were table talk.

So I grew up with the understanding that you don't just say: oh, let's have a synagogue, let's make a place to pray. No, it's not that. It's, "Let's build a place where the full spectrum of human culture, at least its Jewish aspect, can be shared. What does it take to put that together?" And I heard that it takes money, it takes a bank account, it takes lawyers, it takes relationships with the Philadelphia government and the Pennsylvania government, etc. It was there. I was completely aware of it from my earliest recollections.

My father, because of his success there, was invited to become a top administrator in the Jewish Theological Seminary in New York, where he worked with a man who was a genius institution builder, Louis Finkelstein, who I came to know and came to be very close to. Finkelstein was the Chancellor of the Seminary, and he did something unheard of. He took over a tiny rabbinical school—really tiny—which just trained some rabbis, and he had a vision. Again, I heard about his vision around the table at home, and then I got to know him intimately, because I became part of the Seminary culture when my father moved there. Finkelstein's vision was to build the Seminary into a cultural center that spreads its wings far beyond the rabbinical school. And I don't just mean that he included a cantorial school, that he built a world-famous library—the largest Jewish library in the world until the national library in Israel was founded—and collected the premier scholars in every Jewish cultural field. He was also the first person to initiate a cross-cultural conference. He called it the Conference on Science, Philosophy and Religion, which he started in 1939, where he invited top thinkers in various disciplines to come to a conference once a year and to spend four or five days in a retreat in Lake Mohonk, in upstate New York. They would go there every year and he hired an administrator to take care of all the nitty-gritty.

Well in advance they would announce a theme for each conference: what intellectual concept do we want to explore? And everybody who came was expected to prepare a paper. And then everybody would get the papers in advance, they'd read them and then they'd have sessions at which they discussed the various papers in depth. My father was invited to it, and he would always come home glowing about the interactions. It didn't take long for that to become a fashion. It became very common to have interdisciplinary get-togethers, although I don't think a lot of that happens now anymore. It's sort of like a faded idea that people should actually sit down and talk about an idea in depth and actually write papers for other people to talk about in depth. I remember being invited to the last two and then he asked me to be the director of it. But by then the steam had gone out of it.

Mimsy: How old were you when you were invited to the last two?

Dan: I think about 25. It happened around 1960.

Mimsy: And why did he invite you—because your interests were so motley?

Dan: He knew me, we got to know each other. I had a wonderful time, I got to know all these people, I was treated totally respectfully. And I wrote, to me, one of the most interesting papers I ever wrote. At the time I was a physicist and historian and philosopher of science, professionally. And I wrote something called *The Values of Science*, and they discussed it among the other papers.

So these are the kinds of things that I grew up with. And then of course my father's high school buddy was Herman Finkelstein, who went by the nickname of Hinky. And he and Hinky would hang out together often. I got to know him well, and he was a world-class estate lawyer who wrote what at the time was a standard textbook in estate law. He practiced in New York. And his son, Michael, became a good friend of mine.

Mimsy: Are all these Finkelsteins related to each other?

Dan: Yes. Hinky Finkelstein was Lou Finkelstein's brother. And Michael was Hinky's son, and we got very close. Part of my young years was being acquainted with Jewish tradition, which is highly legal; I was a student of Talmud and I studied privately with the greatest scholar of the era, Saul Lieberman, with whom I was very close. And I got to see how a sharp, focused legal mind works and what the difference is when you look at a thing closely and carefully and not just casually. All these things people taught me.

I still remember when Michael Finkelstein first started practicing in a big law firm, and he got his first big case. I said: Michael, I can't wait to read your brief—it was his first big brief, on behalf of the major beer companies. The issue at hand was that they wanted to market a new can of beer that was ten ounces instead of the standard twelve ounces. There was a standard size and they wanted to market a slightly smaller size, obviously to charge the same amount for it and make more money. But it needed government approval. So this was in federal court and he was making the case for the beer companies. He sent me the brief, and this was like a forty page brief with arguments and citations and precedents and decisions all beautifully put together. I loved it, it was like reading a novel for me. I remember calling him up and saying: "Michael, this is so interesting and so well put together. You're bound to win this case." And I still hear his voice on the phone: he burst out laughing. He said, "There's not a chance that I'm going to win this case." I said, "What do you mean? This is so good." He said, "The other side's brief is just as beautiful and they have better arguments." He himself said that. Just that little lesson was so much: you can be clever, but you can still be damn wrong. So these experiences are all part of the way I grew up.

Of course the Talmud is full of such examples. The Rabbis who debated—every one of them was a genius at debate and at reasoning. Unless you've studied it, you have no idea how deep these people were and how they were able to hang onto the slightest hint of something to make a case that sounded really good, until the other side hung out something better—and often the discussion was not even resolved then. So all of these things were part of my world, and then I got into the academic world, and they helped me see what a house of cards that world was in terms of intellect and education.

After I left the academic world, I didn't just walk out. I had a family, I had to feed them. That was the period after Kennedy was elected in 1960 when money started flowing like water into all the sciences, and of course the publishers who publish science textbooks were dancing in the streets. They had money to burn and so they were desperately looking for authors to write books, because everybody was competing for what was now a growing market in textbooks. You can't publish a book unless you have a book! So they would go to universities and ask around for who had a reputation for being good teachers. Somehow, they got to me. They had heard that I made clear presentations, and they said: come on board, write a book for us, and while you're at it (since I told them I was interested in more than that), be an in-house editor. So I got a lucrative book contract to write an introductory physics textbook, which were very profitable at the time, and they thought mine would be too. In addition to that, I was there vetting all kinds of other textbooks that came in, and wining and dining authors at lavish lunches at very fancy restaurants, which was all at government expense—just amazing. We would take a professor out, and the only word I can use to describe it is "slimy". You would take some guy from a major university and treat him to lunch at a restaurant that was hugely expensive and lavish, and already his eyes glistened, there were dollar signs in them, and you won him over just from the lavishness of your hospitality. I saw it close up, I was participating in doing it. I edited a series of books for them—a very fine series of popular books in various fields. I think about ten or fifteen of them came out. So I got to know a lot of people in various fields and what their fields were and a lot of them were my friends from the academic world. I got a lot of experience in the publishing world and I also saw the gritty underside of it, which is that the editors and publishers, the people who actually made the decisions, had no idea what was in their books. I don't even know how they got their positions. They were selling a product that they didn't really understand.

Mimsy: That would have to be true, I guess.

Dan: Of course, if you think about it. So that was a phenomenon in and of itself. But I also learned a lot about the mechanics of publishing, the nitty-gritty mechanics—the copy editing, the galleys, the proofs, how you dealt with print houses, how you sold the books, how you marketed them, how you had to fight for space on shelves. And all the nitty-gritty was, again, part of my everyday life, and totally fascinating. If you're in the publishing world, you get some close up looks at how ideas get disseminated. Back then, it was only through books and magazines. We put out a magazine too!

All of these things gave me glimpses into different worlds, and into different aspects of what makes a total culture that has intellectual and ethical and philosophical foundations.

We talked about the educational aspects of the academic world that turned me off, but there was another thing about the academic world that I was conscious of that really grated on me. And I don't even know where that reaction came from in my background; it certainly didn't come from anything in my surroundings. I had a very strong aversion to hierarchy in society. I'm saying that because I was thrust into the top rungs of it, and never, ever found myself comfortable in it. For example, the academic world is really a rigid hierarchy and you see it in action any time there's a social gathering or any time there's a conference. You are placed in your position in the hierarchy instantaneously when you get there. First of all, there's a rank hierarchy—professor, associate professor, assistant professor, instructor, lecturer—and you know exactly where you stand.

But there's hierarchy among universities, and boy, was I close to that. If you're a professor at Columbia, and someone else is a professor in the same field at NYU, the attitude was: we know who's good and who isn't that good. Columbia's good and NYU is on the second rung. Then there's the internal hierarchy of subject matter within the university community: if you are a professor of physics, well, you're definitely much, much smarter than a professor of chemistry, who outranks biology, or any social science.

Mimsy: Why is that?

Dan: Well, I mean physics is the queen of sciences, it's the exact science.

Mimsy: It is?

Dan: Every other field in the natural sciences is dependent on physics.

Mimsy: There's nothing natural about physics.

Dan: And certainly all of the hard sciences are way above any social sciences. The only thing that *maybe* outranks physics—and this is a debatable matter—is mathematics, because math is abstract, so the question of who's smarter, a physics professor or a math professor, is not easy. If you walk in and say, "I'm a physics professor at Columbia University," they might as well just all bow down and kiss your feet. It's the way it is. You walk into a gathering and the first thing they want to know about you is your rank, your subject and your university and that's how they relate to you. It happens everywhere.

As to people outside the intellectual world, don't even ask. The physical plant guy in the Columbia Physics Department fixed everything, and as far as the people in the department were concerned, he was just a servant. That's all there was to it. Something went wrong: hey, come over here and fix it. Call him up, have him come over. Certainly you weren't going to waste your time in conversation with the guy. And once he fixed it, you said good-bye, see you later. So that always rubbed me the wrong way.

This was also the civil rights movement time, and this was a time when my eyes were opened to some things there too. I was in the March on Washington in 1963, I was there on the mall when Martin Luther King made his famous "I have a dream" speech. A whole bunch of us went down. We came on a bus and it was quite an event. It was really very moving. Everybody was patting themselves on the back about a new era. His message was a hope that people would become color-blind, that color should not be a factor at all, you don't see color. That was his clear message: we're all equal, we're all human beings, we all have to be treated the same way. At Columbia University, everybody was breaking their arms patting themselves on the back at how supportive they were and how they all went down to hear it, and they're all supporting this great new movement.

Three years later in 1966 I was by then living here and I was invited to take a summer job as the director of the science division of a summer program. Harvard University was running a summer program for two months, for professors in black colleges in the South. That's the way it was explained to me. Then the colleges were totally segregated, legally segregated. These were black colleges, and black professors teaching at black colleges were invited to come to Harvard for the summer and be given refresher courses in their fields. The idea was, there they are buried in the South, their universities are poor, so this would give them a chance to rub shoulders with people who are at the forefront of their various professions, at the best university in the world. These visiting professors would be paid a stipend and, of course, all their expenses would be covered. There was to be a program for English, a program for social sciences and a program for science, and I was the one who they chose to be the head of the science division. It sounded like a nice thing, good job, decent pay, at taxpayer expense of course. So I accepted.

There was no orientation or anything. I know what I expected, and what I found was shocking. I found that this "Harvard University" thing was not really Harvard University. It was put together by a bunch of Master's Degree recent graduates in the Harvard Graduate School of Education. Not one of these people even had a doctorate, let alone any degree in their field. None of them. They were young kids whose degrees were in *teaching* school subjects in which they were not expert. They were the ones who designed the subject matter and everything. There was not a single Harvard professor of subject matter involved in this at all.

I looked around. It was the first day. I remember it so vividly. There were all these really magnificent people from southern colleges. They were all senior professors, every one of them. People in their '40s and '50s, a really distinguished group of people, very articulate and very pleasant. They were all there together in anticipation of learning what is new on the cutting edge. I talked to them, and I still didn't know exactly what was going on that first day. The second day was sort of organizational, we talked about different groups, I don't remember the details. But I do remember that by the end of the second afternoon, a wave of fury had descended over this group of professors—I mean *fury*. I was walking around among them, and I was talking to them, and I heard stories like this, from a group of English professors. They said: "What is going on here? These guys are telling us, in the English program, that we shouldn't be teaching Shakespeare to our students, because they're not really capable of understanding that language; that we should be teaching something much more attuned to their capabilities. I've been teaching Shakespeare to my students for 20 years, and they love it. And they're great at it. What is going on here?" I got this close glimpse of the arrogance of the northeastern liberal, who under the guise of being a friend of what they perceived as a wronged minority, actually perceived these people as a second class minority, not deserving of any respect for anything that they've done. That night there was a scheduled meeting of the directors. I lit into them, and I was fired.

Mimsy: Who fired you?

Dan: The director of the whole program. It was the only job I was outright fired from. And I was happy to be fired, I didn't give a damn about their salary. I didn't want to have anything to do with them, or get anywhere near them.

Experiences like that drove me to a passion, a life passion— all of these things I've been recounting of not treating individual human beings the same, even though they're all part of the same human race, they're each whole, human individuals. And that's basically what my book, *The Meaning of Education*, is about. It's about the human individual as an entity of marvel, period. There's no qualifiers. All of these experiences really seared my soul. They were part of me. I was very conscious of it.

Everybody back then talked about "democratic schools"; they still do today, and what they mean by democratic schools has no relationship to what *we* mean by that term. To me the notion of a democratic school was so real and so meaningful, and here I am for fifty years in such a real democratic school, and there's nothing that pleases me more every single day than my ability to interact with people on a one-to-one basis as individual human beings, each with their own individual peculiarities, and to have them, for better or for worse, look at me the same way. They can like me, they can dislike me, they can argue with me, they can be mad, whatever. But we're all *people*. That's the bedrock of the school—without that there's nothing. With that, everything else takes meaning. So that is the passion I brought to it. And it was totally shared by Hanna and by you. I mean you didn't even need it as a discovered passion because you had it. But for me, it was a passion that was born out of experience, and I know you had it, from what I've heard from you, from your upbringing in your home. And Hanna had it from her country, because the whole country was based on that. One of the first people I met when I came to Israel was a street sweeper in Tel Aviv, Steinschneider, who was a well-known philosopher who said: I like to be a street sweeper because it gives me time to think about my philosophical work. This wasn't a put-on.

The next thing I brought to the table was institution building. In 1963, I encountered Jacob Robinson, who changed my life. He was my cousin, but he was also a world-famous historian of the Holocaust, in addition to being a world-famous international legal scholar who was the legal power behind the Eichmann trial, and also an advisor to Justice Jackson, who was a prosecutor in the Nuremberg war crime trials. He was in the top echelons of international law and the international scene in Europe between 1920 and 1940. Later, he was Israel's legal advisor in the U.N. He connected to me because I was in the publishing world, and he had a book he wanted published by a commercial publisher. He had no trouble publishing his works with a Jewish publisher, but he wanted something that would reach a larger audience. Very quickly we became like father and son. I was involved with him and Holocaust studies at a level that's almost unbelievable, from 1963 basically until he died in '77. I actually worked intensively with him for a couple of years on a major book that he wrote, and then after that, on all his articles and research, and I recorded autobiographical interviews with him. Among the things he taught me was that all of history was about *people*. For example, if you read books on the history of the Holocaust, they're almost all sweeping. You get two kinds of genre in the Holocaust literature: you get either personal memoirs, which are very moving and tell you stories of what particular people went through—individuals, their families, their community; or you have sweeping accounts—here, this many people were deported, this many people were gassed, there were experiments done on these people, etc. But what you don't get, because nobody has the scope to get it, is the tremendously subtle differences between the nature of the different Jewish communities to begin with, and more important, the subtle differences between the relation between the Jews and the various local non-Jewish populations throughout Europe. He knew every European language. There's nobody I ever heard of like that. He could read every European language—Hungarian, Finnish, Estonian, all the Slavic languages. He could read them all. He could speak a lot of them. He was totally fluent in at least a dozen languages.

Mimsy: How did he learn them? When did he learn them?

Dan: I know how he learned Danish. He was in the Russian army and he was a prisoner-of-war in the First World War in Denmark. And he had money from rich relatives, and with that money he bribed the guards of the prisoner-of-war camps to bring him newspapers from the outside. He taught himself Danish when he was in Denmark, and translated the Danish newspapers for the other prisoners-of-war who were from Russia. It's very funny because he was actually known as a troublemaker to the German prisoner-of-war camp authorities. They would shuttle him from camp to camp. After he was in a camp for a few months, they'd say: enough of Robinson, move him out of here, send him to another camp. And he'd do the same kind of thing in another camp. He'd bribe people and get underground newspapers and translate them. He never did anything active—he wasn't throwing bombs or trying to escape—but he was causing trouble.

He was phenomenal. He just never, ever settled for sweeping generalities, and he always insisted every community was different, and every situation was different, every interaction among populations was different. The net result was the most horrible crime against humanity ever to happen, but his point was that it wasn't a monolithic thing, and that you must understand that human relations are specific, they're not general. You get a person confronting a person and he's going to beat him or he's going to torture him or he's going to do something else: what you have is two human beings facing each other, doing something to each other. And what they do and what their attitude towards each other is has to do with their backgrounds, their personalities, their culture, their biases, what myths and legends they've been told about each other. If you don't understand that, you'll never comprehend anything. If you see things blindly as just A and B, rather than *person* A and *person* B, you'll never be able to understand the dynamic, or find ways to heal it. He was so clear about that. And he always insisted on understanding human motivations in specific circumstances. That all reinforced my sense of the significance of the individual person in history.

I used to start my history seminars with the same message. There were two things I would always say, and the one thing that is relevant to this discussion is this: I would say, "Look guys, I want you to remember something. When we talk about history, we're going to be talking about *people*. Every single person that I mention historically is just a person, just like you, just like me. They eat, they sleep, they do the normal human functions, they're just like us. So don't look at them as 'historical figures' and give them some mythical proportions. Look at them as people. And if you do that, you'll understand more about history than by looking at them in any other way." I would try to bring a human element into the history seminars, because that's the key. That all came from my background—the people whom I encountered and the mentors that I had. Although they weren't officially mentors, they were mentors—all of them.

So when I ask myself: what did I bring to this enterprise? What I brought to the enterprise was the basic experiential knowledge that building a viable institution involves the full spectrum of different aspects—all of which are interrelated and none of which can be left out if you want the core institution to have life. I guess you could say this is a "systems theory" phenomenon. It's just like putting together a building, or the human body. You know the human body isn't an arm and a leg and a head and a stomach, it's a system that's integrated. And the system that makes up an institution has to do with a lot of things. It has to do with a physical plant, it has to do with the aesthetics of the place, it has to do with the way its governed, the way it handles the people in it, it has to do with the mission statement—what it's there for that has to be clear and deep and based on some solid philosophical grounding. Whether other people agree with it or not, *you* have to agree with it and *you* have to understand the grounding. You can never stop understanding it better. It involves business savvy, it involves money, it involves understanding your relationship with legal forces outside of you that affect you and govern you, and therefor understanding the ins and outs of the law that governs you. All of these things are pieces of putting together an institution.

Usually when you build an institution, you have several different experts who are focusing on each of these fields and trying to work together as a team. I was fortunate in having a lot of these experiences in myself—it just happened. It was accidentally how I was brought up. I was always interested in all of them. Now that I think back on it, I think it was sort of natural—all of it. It was natural, when we put it together, to put together a Board of Trustees of distinguished people; I saw that close up in other places. And the fact that I lived where I did in Framingham just made it easy. I don't know if we could have succeeded if we hadn't had that advantage. We could have landed in that location and wanted to start a school and not had these relationships and not had a school. Another person could be living right where we were in Warren Place and not know the neighbors and have the idea of starting a school in a storefront in South Framingham. I didn't think about it and say: okay, let me see how can I put together a Board of Trustees. I was there, I was amongst the right people, they're people I know, it was natural for me to muster their help. They were responsive because we were interested in one another as friends, without an ulterior motive. We were friends before we talked about a school. Enlisting them for help was a natural thing because that's what you do; I saw that done in other places.

The same goes for everything else. It was clear that you need the best legal advice—I didn't know anything but best legal advice. And the best legal advice has saved us from day one. Time and time again we could have been wiped off the planet without the best legal advice. It's expensive. But you get what you pay for in that world if you choose well. All of these things were clear. You need a budget, you need money. My father used to work on budgets. He would come home and talk about the Seminary's budget. He would talk about money and fundraising and how the budget is short on this and how he had to do this and that. My father at the age of 70 went to the West Coast to Los Angeles and founded the University of Judaism singlehanded there. He got the people together and he got the money, he got everything. The Jewish Theological Seminary sent him out there alone. He didn't have an army of people. And then when he was in his eighties, he did the same thing in Israel. He founded the branch of the Jewish Theological Seminary in Israel, which has become a very distinguished institution in Jerusalem. He knew how to do it.

Mimsy: Actually, it wasn't in his blood.

Dan: That's right, it wasn't. He taught himself. He was an incredible human being who created a master out of very good raw material, out of hard work. It wasn't that hard work for me because I got it, as a gift.

Mimsy: That's a funny way to look at it. I don't think you know what hard work is. You're so used to doing it, you don't even have a clue of what it means.

Dan: None of us got paid anything for the first seventeen years of the school and we all had different ways of putting food on the table, so in the '70s a bunch of us said well, time to find a new way to put food on the table because whatever other sources some of us had had dried up. And other people just thought it would be a good idea. We were all into natural foods by then. Natural foods was beginning to become really fashionable in the '70s.

Mimsy: We were all into it. It was "what you did". It was obviously fashionable.

Dan: There were only a few natural food stores. We had a tiny one around here, which your son famously called the "verbal abuse center", run by Penelope Turton, who was a real pioneer. She created the first organic farm in this whole region in early 1950s, and she was a tough, tough cookie. She was an amazing person, but not the most political person you ever had to interact with.

Mimsy: She got what she wanted.

Dan: So there she was with her little store, and all the natural food stores were these mom and pop operations—very expensive, very small, very limited variety of stuff. So a bunch of us got together and said, "Why not start a natural food supermarket? With volume we'll be able to get prices lower and have more variety and people will probably flock to it." If you think back on it, we were ten years ahead of the curve on it—we know that now.

Mimsy: It ain't nothin' compared to being a hundred years ahead of the curve on schooling.

Dan: That's right. But we didn't know how many years. So there we were with this new idea. There was no other natural food supermarket in the country. There were no models, there was nothing to follow. And just like with the school, we had very little money to play with. We raised money amongst ourselves, and it was really very little. We rented a place on Route 9, and got incorporated with one of the lawyers who had been associated with the school. We called ourselves "The Natural Grocer"—nice name. We worked very hard, and put together all the little pieces with a shoestring. One of the people involved in The Natural Grocer, for example, was Paul Wilson, an SVS grad, who was a legendary genius at putting together machines. He helped us put together the freezers and all the hardware, the automatic food packagers for bulk food packaging, and so forth. And we got catalogs of distributors. You have no idea how funny that was in so many ways, because the wholesalers to these mom and pop stores did volumes equivalent to that of one store today.

Mimsy: Yes, that's right. And yet they had pretty fancy catalogs.

Dan: Yes, catalogs were easy to put together. We put one together too. And we learned a lot about the mechanics of that industry later, but I don't want to go into that. The point is that here we were, and institution building was just part of what we did. So, we put together a supermarket. We had all the pieces—the legal side, the money, the rental, the physical plant, the parts that went into it, hired the people. We published literature, just like the school published it. We advertised in newspapers, just like the school did back then. All of our experience was brought to bear on this and we had a beautiful store. We opened on May 10 of 1977. Everybody was very excited about it. That was a historic date, because that was one of the latest big snowstorms ever recorded in Massachusetts—six to eight inches of snow fell on that day. It put quite a damper on our opening day!

The store was a rousing success in the beginning. We did a lot of business—so much so that eventually we opened a chain of five supermarkets, in Cambridge, Chelmsford, Brookline and Burlington.

It was all part of institution building. We were into that. People involved in the school had that talent. We knew what to do because we knew how to put the different pieces together that are so varied and have so many sides to them, so many negotiations, so many things with the health department and authorities and this and that and the other thing. We weren't just a group of people off the street who said: oh, let's put together a supermarket. We were a group of people who said: we know how to do this, we know how to build an institution, we'll build one. We built a school, we'll build a natural food supermarket. That's what we had. I brought a lot of that to the table. You perfectly fit in with it. And we managed to do that.

That's what has kept the school going, that founding core—those three people who carried the school for fifty years—brought a panoply of talents and skills and experiences and life experiences, all of which together were relevant to creating an integrated system where all of the facets were covered with a lot of knowledge and a lot of life experience. That's what has stood us in good stead. Hopefully the young staff who are in the school now will have absorbed it by the time a few more years go by, just like we absorbed it.

Everything we did was the same: What a crazy idea for a school like ours to create the Sudbury Valley School Press. I mean it's insane. The Sudbury Valley School Press has probably done 3 or 4 hundred thousand dollars worth of business since it first was created—sold books all over the world, made us known everywhere. We have a PR campaign that obviously has made us known everywhere. You and I sat and planned a PR campaign in 1985. We did it with $20,000 from a total reserve fund of $50,000 that the school had at the time, and we convinced the school to spend on this gamble, which brought the school from an unsteady 70 to 80 students to over 100 very quickly, and put the school on the map. Just conceiving stuff like that is something. You have to have that confidence that you can put together all the facets that are required. We didn't really have that much experience in PR, but we knew about PR. We developed a taste for PR through The Natural Grocer. Clearly, that was our first introduction. And that served us in good stead when we started our PR campaign. All of my experience in publishing helped us. We were tempted when we started putting out our first books to try to have them published by a commercial publishing house, and we probably could have. But my experience came into play because I knew that the world of publishing is such that this was going to be a very doubtful way of getting our message out, clearly. So we said no, we're going to create our own publishing house, and we did it. We printed books, we distributed them, we had catalogs, we did all the things that you have to do. It was part of what we brought to the institution.

That has been the key, and I think the reason we're still here after 50 years. Among the three of us, we've had these life experiences from our upbringing, from our training, from our lives, that together we have created an integrated system that is perfect for institution building. And we expect that the people who are growing up with it will enable the school to continue to thrive, because they will have absorbed those experiences, partially from their own life experiences, and also from their experience at the school.